Typhoon Pilot

Group Captain D. J. Scott, DSO, OBE, DFC and Bar, is one of New Zealand's most famous war heroes. During the war he commanded 486 New Zealand Squadron flying mainly from Tangmere in southern England. The squadron was originally equipped with Hurricanes but eventually changed to flying Typhoons. Later he commanded 123 Wing – four RAF squadrons of Rocket-Firing Typhoons – in the campaigns in northern Europe. At 25, he was the youngest Group Captain in the Allied Air Force and the only member of the RNZAF to command a mobile wing during Operation Overlord.

He has the unique distinction of being decorated by every country in which he served, holding the Croix de Guerre and Palm from France, the Croix de Guerre and Palm from Belgium and from Holland the Commander of the Order of Orange Nassau.

Desmond Scott lives in Christchurch, New Zealand.

Typhoon Pilot

Group Captain
DESMOND SCOTT

DSO, OBE, DFC and Bar, Commander
Orange Nassau, French Croix de Guerre
and Palm, Belgian Croix de Guerre
and Palm, MID

ARROW BOOKS

Arrow Books Limited
62–65 Chandos Place, London WC2N 4NW

An imprint of Century Hutchinson Limited

London Melbourne Sydney Auckland
Johannesburg and agencies throughout
the world

First published in Great Britain by Leo Cooper in
association with Martin Secker & Warburg Ltd 1982
Arrow edition 1987

Printed and bound in Great Britain by
Anchor Brendon Limited, Tiptree, Essex

ISBN 0 09 950700 5

Contents

Illustrations

Note: Photographs marked IWM in the 8 page section are reproduced by permission of the Imperial War Museum.

Foreword

by

Air Vice-Marshal W. J. Crisham, CB, CBE, RAF (Rtd.)

This is a story about heroes, a record of their collective courage and skill, alight with the fierce enthusiasm of their young leader, Desmond Scott.

Scottie—himself a brilliantly able and magnificent pilot—forged his closely-knit team of young New Zealand pilots into a superb fighting unit, capable of meeting constantly changing operational needs with matchless efficiency.

Scottie's operations, whether he was squadron commander or wing leader, bore the stamp of immaculate planning and execution. He was always concerned for the safety of his pilots and other aircrew, especially those who had the misfortune to be 'downed' in the sea. Indeed, his rescue operations dangerously close to the enemy coast were cast in the heroic mould and gave a tremendous boost to morale.

The Tangmere Typhoons were extremely active during the build-up prior to the Normandy invasion, primarily in the neutralization of flying bomb and other missile-launching sites, and later in the destruction of heavily defended radar stations before D-Day. These vital tasks were successfully carried out.

On the Normandy bridgehead, with Scottie and his Tangmere Typhoon squadrons now in the Second Tactical Air Force, the rocket-firing Typhoons smashed the enemy's tanks and road convoys at Falaise and hustled him homewards via the Channel Ports and the Scheldt Estuary to the Rhine.

The job was done!
To the dauntless nothing is denied.

W. J. Crisham

Introduction

Whereas the Spitfire always behaved like a well-mannered thorough-bred, on first acquaintance the Typhoon reminded me of a half-draught: a low-bred cart horse, whose pedigree had received a sharp infusion of hot-headed sprinter's blood. It lacked finesse, and was a tiger to argue. Mastering it was akin to subduing the bully in a bar-room brawl. Once captured, you held a firm rein, for getting airborne was like riding the wild wind. One casual crack of the whip, and the jockey was almost left behind. But like the human race, the Typhoon had its good points too. In sharing the dangerous skies above Hitler's Europe I had good reason to respect its stout-hearted qualities. It gave no quarter; expected none. It carried me into the heart of the holocaust—and even when gravely wounded delivered me from its flames. As a young pilot I grew not only to respect the Typhoon, but also to trust—even to love—it.

After the death of the Third Reich, silently and unobtrusively the Typhoons flew off in obscurity. But I shall never forget them. Not ever, for by the war's end they had become part of me.

The travels of Desmond Scott and his New Zealand Squadrons.

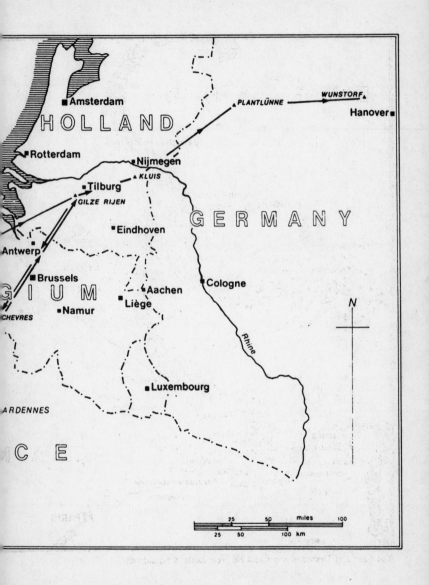

Prologue

I was brought up with horses, and it was therefore only natural, when I left grammar school, that I joined the Territorial Army and became a trooper in our Canterbury Yeomanry Cavalry. The rattle of spurs, the mature conversation of older men and the orchestrated performance of our horses, was a welcome change from the classroom, but life in the cavalry had its sore points too, as I was quick to learn.

One day while on manoeuvres, our troop was 'attacked' by two Bristol Fighter planes, ancient relics of the First World War, and flown by pilots of the New Zealand Air Force. As they swooped low over our heads, my horse, which normally had the heart of a lion, took the bit in his teeth and bolted. One of the pilots, savouring my predicament, persistently pressed home his 'attacks' and, several fences and a few ditches later, Toby and I parted company. To add insult to injury, I received an impolite hand signal from above, and decided there and then, if I was to fight my wars in a sitting position I would need a steed that could not only fly, but outsprint any opposition.

When our annual camp disbanded, I began taking flying lessons in an Aero Club Gypsy Moth, but in those days dual instruction was 30 shillings an hour, and consequently my progress was expensive and slow. However, after a total of six and a half hours dual instruction, I managed to go solo, and was saved from my creditors by a stroke of good forturne. Just prior to Hitler's indiscretions, our government introduced a scheme in which successful applicants were given 40 hours flying at the taxpayer's expense. Much to my surprise, my application was successful. About the same time that I had completed my 40 hours, England declared war on Germany. I promptly received a registered letter from our Air Department reminding me of a small clause at the bottom of our contract. Thus I was compelled to leave the cavalry and became a member of His Majesty's Junior Service, but it was not until August, 1940, and after much flying in antiquated Fairey Gordons, that I finally set sail for the other side of the world to take my place among the survivors of Churchill's 'few'.

Flying Hurricanes was a far cry from piloting slow old biplanes, but again I was lucky, for my first operational posting was to the Orkney Islands, a relatively quiet area in Hitler's blitz. A few weeks protecting part of the British Fleet at Scapa Flow gave me the opportunity to gain the necessary experience that helped me to survive in No 11 Group, the RAF's hot spot, which included London and most of the south coast. It was in this prestigious company that I spent the following four years.

Hurricanes were already the work horse of Fighter Command and for nearly two years I piloted them on almost every type of operation. There were many nights when I flew above a burning London. I participated in daylight shipping attacks along the French and Belgian coasts and acted as close escort to Blenheim and Stirling bombers, on raids that were aptly code-named 'Circuses'. I survived a mid-air collision with one of No 23 Squadron's Havocs, and it was also from a long-range Hurricane that I watched Cologne explode, as a thousand RAF bombers emptied their war load from the night sky. As with our adversaries, our offensive operations were often more spectacular than successful. Nonetheless, all were hazardous, and the experience gained by those who survived was always sorely won.

When I had completed the equivalent of two operational tours, I began to feel the strain and did not object when I was promoted to Squadron Leader and posted on rest to a temporary staff appointment at Bentley Priory, the headquarters of Fighter Command.

1

Bentley Priory

No sane pilot would have wanted a posting to a Typhoon squadron in the winter of 1942. New types of aircraft always had their faults, but the Typhoon had far more than most. For a start, its huge 24-cylinder Napier Sabre liquid-cooled engine was far from dependable. If it stopped dead while you were in the air, you were faced with two alternatives—over the side, or the gliding angle of a seven-ton brick. Even worse was its tail section. For reasons which even the experts could not fathom, several Typhoons had shed their tails and buried themselves and their pilots in very deep holes.

Nonetheless, there was something about this all-metal aircraft which rather appealed to me. It had a very determined chin, its 20 mm Hispano cannons stuck out like ramrods, and its gigantic three-bladed propeller gave it a pugnacious air which few other aircraft of its time possessed. Head on, it was not unlike a bulldog. But unlike a bulldog it could outsprint anything that had so far flown in the European or any other theatre.

I had already completed two tours in the Typhoon's elder brother, the much smaller Hawker Hurricane. This gentle saviour of Britain was a beautiful aircraft to fly, by day or by night, but at this stage of the war it was rapidly being phased out of the European theatre for service in the desert and Far East air forces, where the opposition was less formidable. It was still quite capable on anti-flak missions, but it could not longer hold its own alongside the latest Spitfires, and it was no fun for the pilot of a Hurricane suddenly to feel he was flying backwards when he tangled with a Messerschmitt 109 or Focke Wulf 190.

In the Typhoon—with all its faults—I could see a ray of hope. If Hawkers could build the dependable Hurricane then they must be

1

capable—once the faults were ironed out—of turning out something similar in its younger and much faster brother. So I set my sights on a Typhoon squadron, and began plotting to escape from my temporary staff job at Bentley Priory, the headquarters of Fighter Command.

The Priory, once the home of Nelson's mistress, Emma Hamilton, was situated in the London suburb of Stanmore. Its cold stone walls hid a hive of industry, so all operational pilots naturally avoided it. Operational squadron life, although dangerous at times, was free and easy and in sharing the fortunes of war we relied so much on one another that differences just did not exist, and we jealously guarded this happy state of affairs from every intrusion. However, it was Command practice to post to the Priory certain tour-expired officers, in the hope they would help the chairborne types to 'keep up with the field'. Being posted to the Priory was like being sent from the follies to the morgue. The only redeeming feature was that it was within easy distance of the great metropolis, with its wide and varied range of attractions.

The Command's regular staff were not all Air Force officers. Many senior First World War naval and army officers were there on liaison duties for their respective services. Having spent a good part of my early operational life blasting my way into enemy shipping, I soon grew impatient with two old naval captains who persisted in re-fighting the 26-year-old Battle of Jutland on the mess bar. Fortunately the army officers were not so boring, but after their retreat from Dunkirk they appeared to have little if anything to talk about. However, I did feel sorry for an elderly brigadier-general—after I had nearly killed him! He was not a member of the staff but was visiting the Priory and had asked me if I would consider flying him over his old tank regiment which was on manoeuvres near Framlingham in Suffolk. My heart softened when he confided that he had served alongside New Zealanders in the First World War, and after a drink too many I agreed to meet him the following morning at Martlesham Heath.

I selected a Miles Magister, a low-wing monoplane with two very open cockpits, one set some distance behind the other and connected by a simple voice tube, like a vacuum cleaner hose, into which we also plugged our earphones. Before helping him into the rear cockpit, where I considered he would command the better bird's-eye view, I enquired whether he had ever flown before, and received the haughty reply that he had been airborne before I was even chair-borne.

I strapped him in and we were soon off into the cold, rough morning air, flying low over the Suffolk woodlands in search of his troops. A freshening in the wind did not help, and the little aircraft began to flip and flop like a puppet on a string. The general did not complain, and I carried on, executing steep turns to the left followed by figure eights to the right, fairly close to the tree tops. After about half an hour I was feeling cold and asked my passenger if he had spotted any tanks in the woods yet. There was no reply, and I assumed that his earphones had become detached.

As I banked again to the left I looked round—not easy when your neck is frozen stiff. The general appeared to dive half out of the cockpit as if to retrieve something from the underbelly of the aircraft. This also happened when I banked over to the right. He flopped over in that direction like a rag doll, and when I straightened up on to an even keel, his head and arms remained vertical, as if he were hanging upside down.

I could see all was not well and hurried back to land at Martlesham Heath. He was unconscious and had lost his helmet and his false teeth. The ground staff helped me lower him to the grass and I was greatly relieved when an ambulance arrived and a medical orderly pronounced him still alive. He was carted off to the station sick quarters, conscious but suffering from severe shock

I don't think any of us temporary staff officers left our mark in the annals of Command staff history. Not having distinguished myself at school, the mess bar was the only place where I could hold my own with the Oxbridge dons who pushed their pens in pursuit of victory. However, I did have the dubious distinction of being the only officer to be ordered from the Command conference room. This happened during a high-powered conference on operational policy, and at which only two of us present had actually flown operationally during the flying under discussion.

This conference was to evaluate plans to help Bomber Command in its early saturation raids on the Ruhr. Wing Commander Sammy Hoare, my contemporary, sat opposite to me in the lowly seats allotted to us at the far end of the table. Both Sammy and I had done a lot of offensive night work and I wanted to suggest that the RAF should cover all German night fighter bases during the raids, even if it meant calling on Training Command and our light day bomber forces. I knew from experience that it did not take much to upset our night traffic control if our airfields were visited by German intruder patrols. No pilot could concentrate on shooting down bombers when he was told by his ground control that his base was being patrolled by the enemy, was covered in craters and delayed-action bombs, and worse still that all neighbouring airfields were receiving the same treatment.

It was up to Sammy, senior to me in rank, to speak first. But he just sat, twiddling his moustache, his eyes far away in the clouds. However, as the meeting was about to close, there came a familiar voice from the far end of the conference table: 'What do you think, Squadron Leader Scott?' It belonged to one of our great war leaders, Air Marshal Sir Trafford Leigh-Mallory. Two rows of balding heads on either side of the table turned my way and it took me a moment or two to collect myself and blurt out a reply:

'I don't—Sir! This plan you are adopting is a lot of cock!'

There was dead silence. Then the Air Marshal pointed a finger at the door, which thankfully was at my end of the room, and thundered 'Out!'

I made for the door with my head held high, but my discomfiture was not yet complete. There was a blackboard and easel to the side of my line of flight and, my left foot just clipped its base, I tripped and shot through the door almost before opening it. If someone had laughed or even sniggered it might not have seemed so bad, but there was total silence. I slammed the door shut as soon as I was through— much swifter than was necessary.

I still like to believe that this brief encounter with my Commander-in-Chief had a happy and fruitful outcome. A few days later another conference was called. Although I was not present, I had submitted my thoughts on paper and these ideas were adopted almost to the letter. When they were put into practice the percentage of our Bomber Command losses dropped, and remained that way until the German air force was able to invent more sophisticated aids for its night fighter operations.

Two years later, when I was commanding a mobile wing of rocket-firing Typhoons on the Normandy bridgehead, I was to meet Trafford Leigh-Mallory again, only on this occasion I inadvertently ordered him off my airfield.

My leg was in plaster at the time, having been broken a few weeks earlier. The dusty airstrip near Bayeaux was busy as my four squadrons of Typhoons were taking off and landing in a continuous procession. In the midst of all the noise and dust a little Beaver-type communication aircraft landed on to the runway, and wildly waving a crutch at its pilot, I told him to take his bloody toy else-where. With an air of resignation he pointed down towards the cabin, and there through the thick Normandy dust I could see Sir Trafford. I almost dropped a crutch while attempting to salute, and we quickly led his aircraft to a quieter spot near the marshalling area.

We saw one another quite frequently after that, and I became rather fond of him in a distant sort of way. It was at Merville airfield, near Lille in the Pas de Calais, that we met for the last time. He was relinquishing his position as Commander-in-Chief of the Allied Expeditionary Air Forces and called in to say goodbye before flying out to the Far East in a York aircraft of Transport Command. Regrettably, it flew into a mountain and all aboard were killed.

Before leaving the shelter of Bentley Priory I was almost shot down—and in a most undignified way. We usually made sure that we were not always confined to our desks and often flew far and wide on visits to the many stations of Fighter Command. I even attended two RAF station parties, 200 miles apart, in one night. And if the Windmill girls were performing at a certain station, we always found good reason to be there.

Our own communication flight was at nearby Northolt and con-sisted of an assorted collection of small unarmed prewar aircraft such as Proctors and Vega Gulls. After a rugged night attending a party at Westhampnett with the New Zealand Spitfire pilots of 485 Squad-ron, during which I was filled with whisky and canned New Zealand oysters, I climbed into a Vega Gull to fly back to Northolt. My way was blocked by thick cloud over the hills behind Arundel, so there was no alternative but to break the rules and fly up the coast in the direction of Ramsgate in the hope of making my way home via the Thames Estuary. No unarmed aircraft was permitted to fly in the vicinity of the south coast because of the many Luftwaffe low-level fighter bomber raids that were taking place at that time. FW 190s and Me 109s would fly in low, drop their bombs, and after straffing the streets of the coastal towns make off back to France before our own fighters could scramble off and intercept.

Nursing a fierce hangover and near Hastings flying just below the cloud base at about 600 ft, I suddenly noticed several large explosions below and to starboard. Almost simultaneously, four yellow-nosed Me 109s zoomed up after me from near ground level. As a stream of tracer sped past me I yanked back hard on the stick and beat the next burst into cloud only by a bare margin. Feeling like a rabbit that had just made his hole an inch ahead of the terriers, I flew around in cloud for what seemed an eternity, but as soon as I poked my nose out I received a burst from our own friendly anti-aircraft gunners below. In no position to stay and argue, I was forced to fly in cloud until well out to sea before letting down into broken fog and making my way over the waves towards Ramsgate, hoping I would not run into the Royal Navy.

I made my landfall near Deal, and flew up and down just off the coast waggling my wings frantically to make sure that every gunner could see I was a British pilot in trouble and begging for friendly recognition. But I was not so lucky. As I crossed in low between Deal and Sandwich I received a hot reception from small arms fire, and discovered after landing at Manston that parts of my Vega Gull resembled a colander. Since we did not wear chutes in those prewar aircraft, I could only mop my brow and utter a thankful prayer.

Getting myself clear of Fighter Command HQ at Bentley Priory was difficult. Air Marshal Leigh-Mallory was determined that each tour-expired pilot posted to his HQ for temporary staff duties would spend a full six months there before returning to operations. On reflection I suppose he was right, but at that time I could have thought of many happier ways of resting from operations. The Luftwaffe pilots had the advantage over us when it came to resting from the strain of operational flying. They had a variety of choices—from skiing in the Harz mountains to sunbathing and swimming in the Mediterranean. We had no choice, but just stayed in Britain and busied ourselves in some way towards the conduct of war. However, a couple of weeks fishing in Scotland would have been more beneficial to me than six months at Fighter Command HQ.

Comparatively speaking, the Priory was a safe place. But it lacked the squadron spirit and we all longed to be back on operations. For a time I saw a channel of escape when Squadron Leader Don Parker, whose office I shared, was returning to Bomber Command. Don had friends on the staff at High Wycombe, Bomber Command's HQ, and he considered there was a good chance of arranging a posting for me to a multi-engine squadron, where I would be his second pilot until I became proficient enough to have my own aircraft. Although I did not know at the time, Don did his work well. Within a few days of his departure from the Priory I was asked to report to my

Commander-in-Chief and old opponent of the conference table—Air Marshal Sir Trafford Leigh-Mallory.

I arrived on time at his office and sat waiting to be ushered in to his presence. As the mantel clock slowly ticked off the minutes, I could not help noticing a familiar wartime poster. It spelt out the message 'Walls Have Ears!' I was just thinking this was a bit unnecessary when a buzzer sounded and I was taken before the great man himself. Looking resplendent at his throne-like desk, Sir Trafford greeted me like a long-lost friend and disarmingly complimented me on my efforts as a staff officer and on my valuable contributions to the general well-being of his command. But if he could build a person up, he could take him to pieces with equal efficiency. It soon became clear that the old fellow had intercepted my posting notice and did not think much of my efforts to desert him for Bomber Command.

However, I did not think my wishes were anything to be ashamed of, and in contrast to the confrontation in the conference room, I was able to stand my ground, if somewhat shakily. I informed him that I was wasting my time at Bentley Priory, and that it would be better for all concerned if I were back on operations—Bomber, Coastal or Fighter—it did not matter which. My arguments appeared to find a chink in his armour, for he suddenly began lecturing me like a benevolent godfather. Of course I could go back on operations. In fact I would be taking over 486 (NZ) Typhoon Squadron, based at Tangmere—just as soon as my six months' staff appointment was up!

As I left his room and hurried off in the direction of the mess bar, I felt a strong urge to do hand stands. I had still a further six weeks to serve at the Priory, but at least I knew where I was going. A few days later Don Parker was reported missing, believed killed. His was the only aircraft to be shot down from a small force which had raided a target in northwest Germany. So, unknowingly, Sir Trafford had saved my skin.

Many of my contemporaries at the Priory who had returned to operations had already been killed or posted as missing, but after the heavy losses of squadron life one just learned to accept it. Of course the young hopeful who always set the bar alight, who was the ring-leader in every prank hatched at the Priory, was missed for a time. But his loss was passed off as lightly as possible, for he had lived his life to the full, and if it had to end, that is the way he would have wanted it.

I did, however, feel sad for Richard Hillary when he was killed in a Beaufighter soon after his return to flying. Richard had been a frequent visitor to our mess at the Priory, where his presence was a constant reminder of what might happen to any of us. I would often find him sitting alone, his red-rimmed eyes staring into space, completely oblivious of our comings and goings. He had been shot down during the Battle of Britain and had lost his face and most of his fingers in the worst case of burns I had seen up to that time. Although Sir Archibald McIndoe and his team of plastic surgeons had done their best, I could never talk freely with Richard for any length of time for fear of saying the wrong thing. I had a strong feeling, even then, that the proud spirit which had set his young life afire was still burning bravely deep down in his tortured soul, and that he was forever yearning to get back into the skies which had treated him so harshly.

I often longed for the warm brown hills of North Canterbury in far off New Zealand, where I had spent many of the happiest of my boyhood days. However, for most of my RAF contemporaries the night spots of London drew them like powerful magnets and, providing they were solvent, the Priory seldom saw much of them during the hours of darkness. All were English except Johnny Kent, a likeable Canadian who held a regular commission in the RAF and had made a name for himself in the Battle of Britain.

I was junior in both age and rank to most of them, but it was a case of either tagging along or being left back at the Command mess to share my evenings with the permanent chairborne staff, the bar room bores or the Command's intellectuals.

So generally about half a dozen of us would board the tube at Stanmore for the 30-minute ride to London's West End.

Our first call was as always Shepherds in the Haymarket, hosted by Oscar, a genial Swiss. This little corner pub became a permanent gathering place for most of us who served in the RAF and were in striking distance of London. Oscar was extremely kind to his 'Air Force boys', as he called us. Often too kind, for he once showed me a pile of dishonoured Air Force cheques which, had they been presented to the drawers' commanding officers, might well have triggered off a series of court martials severe enough to have affected adversely the war against Germany. Most were for only small sums, but together they totalled a sizeable amount. I asked Oscar why he did not try to recover some of his losses; he merely shrugged his shoulders answering that he accepted it as part of his war effort.

The Savoy in the Strand was also a popular port of call, although we normally went there only on special occasions, such as birthdays, promotions, or after visiting Buckingham Palace. I was taken to White's, one of the most exclusive clubs in England, by one of the Purdy Brothers of South Audley Street, the makers of the finest shotguns in the world. Entering White's was like stepping back into the early part of the nineteenth century. The smoke-stained walls hung with dark portraits of Gladstone and Disraeli were rather depressing, and drinking champagne from battered old pewter mugs added further to the distance between the present and the past.

It was at White's that I met an army captain called Lyttelton who reminded me of Sir Francis Drake before the approach of the Spanish Armada. He was undoubtedly an English aristocrat. With Germany and the British Empire at each other's throats in a life and death struggle, here was a man who spoke nostalgically of cricket! Many years later I was to meet him again, this time in New Zealand as Lord Cobham, then my country's most popular Governor-General.

One of my favourite eating places was Bentley's oyster bar in Albemarle Street. Back home in New Zealand oysters were about a shilling a dozen on shell, yet I had never tasted a raw oyster until I was introduced to Bentley's. After downing two dozen and a large quantity of draught stout I was staggered to learn they were 30 shillings a dozen, then the equivalent of a day's pay. But I became addicted to them and we always lunched at Bentley's when in London.

Leaving Bentley's one day we came across a driverless Austin taxi, with its engine still running, parked outside the door. It was one of the old cabriolet type with folded-down canvas hood and a glass partition between the back seat and the driver. I told Cam Malfroy and Dereck Walker, both wing commanders, to hop in the back while I took my place at the wheel and by pushing and crashing the great gear lever into the required slots, we made a hasty but noisy exit from Albemarle Street. As we drove down the Strand I looked around and found Dereck standing up in the back, his forelock pulled down over his forehead, and his right arm outstretched in a passable imitation of Adolf Hitler. Most of the Londoners on the pavements gave us a rousing reception, but I noticed their sentiments were not shared by some of the older Colonel Blimps who were a permanent part of the London street scene at that time.

Soon afterwards Dereck married Diana Barnarto, a well-known ATA pilot. Sadly he met his death within days of their marriage and

with his passing the Royal Air Force lost one of its most popular
practical jokers.

The last few days at Fighter Command HQ reminded me of my final
days as a boarder at Cathedral Grammar School, Christchurch. I was
pleased to be leaving, yet the sombre good wishes of the regular staff
were a constant reminder of future uncertainties.

Aircraft were much like human beings—some popular, others the
opposite. Many exciting battles were fought over again in the mess
bar by the pilots of Spitfires, Hurricanes and Mosquitoes. But as soon
as the newcomer, the Hawker Typhoon, was mentioned, a deathly
hush descended, as if a judge had just donned his black cap and was
about to pass sentence. However, in spite of its bad reputation, and
the fact that I had not yet flown one, for some reason the Typhoon
did not frighten me. On the contrary, I had a feeling we were to
become good friends.

2

Tangmere

I arrived at RAF station Tangmere in the spring of 1943. As I eased myself out of the staff car which brought me from the control tower to the officers' mess, I noticed snowdrops skirting the driveway, already nodding their last farewells, and daffodils about to bloom in profusion under the mess windows around the nearby tennis courts. Apart from the distant growl of Typhoons labouring in the sick bays near their squadron dispersal huts, the whole world seemed at peace. I suddenly remembered it was the first day of April.

I had landed at Tangmere a number of times during my previous operational tours and was no stranger to the officers' mess. Also I had flown down from Bentley Priory in the course of my staff duties and to attend occasional officers' mess parties. Although Tangmere was sorely mauled during the Battle of Britain, the mess itself had lost only one wing. Built well before the outbreak of war it was more dignified than palatial, and its warm brick walls transmitted a feeling of homely security. As I stepped into the entrance hall I had a strong feeling that I already belonged. And when from the bar I heard the unmistakable drawl of New Zealand voices, I knew I was home.

My bedroom upstairs in the east wing was a pleasant room with a view of the spire of Chichester Cathedral. Beyond that, though not visible, lay the south coast and the English Channel. The room was certainly not overfurnished, but contained all the necessities, including a washbasin with a square mirror above it. This may well have framed a thousand young faces, but I preferred to start afresh, so I placed it upside down in the bottom of the wardrobe where it could rest alone with its memories. In its place I hung a small stainless steel mirror, the gift of a kind wellwisher before I had left New

Zealand. Stuck on its bottom edge was a brief but haunting message:
'Smile, and the Lord Smiles With You.'

Shaving in the mornings or dressing for the evening mess, I always
did my best to answer my mirror's humble prayer; but I must say
there were times in the past, and no doubt there would be in the
future, when my reflection would become hidden or distorted behind
tears. Like most other combat pilots, I was always a bit apprehensive,
and the more operations I survived the more superstitious I became.
After two years of operational flying, sunrise and sunset were no
longer just the start and finish of each day. They were the beginning
and end to another chapter in my life, and I saw in each a beauty and
warmth which hitherto I had failed even to notice.

As I continued to unpack, there was a gentle tapping at the door.
I was expecting my batman, but it turned out to be an attractive
WAAF.

'Yes,' I said. 'What can I do for you?'

'I'm your batman, sir,' she replied.

'You mean batwoman!'

'Yes sir, batwoman.'

As she helped me to finish unpacking, my surprise turned to
embarrassment, for in a last-minute rush before leaving the Priory
I had thrown in my dirty washing, including some pink woollen
underclothes which my mother had sent from New Zealand to
keep me warm during the winter of 1940. They had become rather
holey by this time, but my batwoman did not comment, so I guess
she thought they were possibly part of my flying kit—which in some
ways was true.

After everything was put away, and that didn't amount to very
much, she asked me the usual questions: 'Do you like an early cup of
tea, sir? Milk, sir? How many sugars, sir? Will you be like most of the
other officers and wear battle dress for evening mess?'

This last question pulled me up with a jolt, and it took some
seconds for me to reply: 'No, certainly not. Unless under special
operational circumstances, for which you will be advised, I shall
always require my uniform for evening mess, and so will other
members of my New Zealand squadron. What the other three
squadrons do is their affair.'

Slightly taken aback, she excused herself, picked up my washing,
including my pink long johns, and hurried out of the room to spread
my unhappy tidings among the rest of the mess staff.

After a wash and brush up I wandered downstairs and looked in at the bar, deserted except for a padre and a young pilot officer in the distinctive dark blue uniform of the Royal Australian Air Force. I glanced into the anteroom. The sole occupant was a white bull terrier asleep in front of the fire.

Entering the dining hall was like going into another world, and a busy and noisy one. However, the hum and chatter stopped suddenly as a hundred pairs of eyes looked in my direction. For a moment I felt as though I were facing a jury, but as soon as I took my seat at one of the tables, the murmur of many voices and the clatter of crockery and cutlery resumed as quickly as it had ceased.

As I tackled a virtually inedible cold meat pie, I noticed a bevy of neat and attractive WAAF waitresses near the servery clearly discussing the new arrival—it was always the best looking girls who were chosen to serve at the tables in every officers' mess. Then I saw some familiar faces, one in particular taking me away back to Levin, in the North Island of New Zealand, where we had both started our air force training on the same day. Flying Officer Lyndon Griffiths had not changed much. He still looked the big overgrown kid who had left his school desk and walked smiling straight into a dangerous future. On the other hand, Flight-Lieutenant Harvey Sweetman, who had served earlier with 485 New Zealand Spitfire Squadron, looked tired and much older than when I had last seen him several months earlier.

After lunch I made my way into the anteroom where two stewards were serving coffee. Griffiths and Sweetman were the first to greet me, followed by a number of the 486 New Zealand Typhoon Squadron. 'Griff' belonged to one of the Spitfire squadrons on the other side of the aerodrome, but Harvey was one of the flight commanders in 486. He introduced me to Flight-Lieutenants Arthur 'Spike' Umbers of Dunedin, Taylor-Cannon, nicknamed 'Hyphen', and Jim McCaw, a farmer from the Hakataramea Valley in North Otago. Also present was Frank Murphy of Wellington, the glamour boy of A Flight, whose younger brother Stan had been one of my classmates in training at Wigram.

Before making my presence felt about the station it was essential to pay my respects to the station commander, Group Captain Hector McGregor, a tall, spare New Zealander who came from Hawkes Bay and had joined the RAF in 1928. He was not only my senior in rank but also by several years and, like many prewar New Zealand regulars, had become more English than the English.

Some days before leaving Fighter Command HQ I had been invited to Uxbridge to lunch with my new group commander, Air Vice-Marshal Sir Hugh Saunders, Tangmere being one of the airfields in his No 11 Group. 'Ding' Saunders was a First World War ace and during the 1930s had been Chief of Staff of the RNZAF in Wellington, so New Zealanders were no strangers to him. He always welcomed an opportunity to discuss any operational problems or new ideas with his squadron and wing leaders, and I had told him that I though 486 Squadron was being wasted in a solely defensive role. Intercepting a few low-level sneak raiders from time to time was not my idea of an all-out effort to win the war. I felt that the squadron could be far better employed on the offensive, without neglecting any of its present commitments. Before I left him at Uxbridge, he had given me a free hand to do whatever I wished with the squadron, providing our operations over the Continent did not clash with the general pattern of the group's offensive.

Acting on this knowledge, during my interview with Group Captain McGregor I indicated that I would be taking my squadron on to the offensive just as soon as I could prepare its pilots for their new role. He sharply reminded me that he was Sector Commander, and any change in plans would be at his discretion and not at mine. Of course I could not tell him that our AOC had given me a free hand, nor would it have been to my advantage to argue. Somewhat deflated, I left his office knowing that our association had not got off to a good start. However, I need not have worried for a week or two later he was posted out to the Lebanon.

486 Squadron was stationed on the west side of the airfield, with some two or three hundred yards separating A and B dispersals. After making myself known to the Tangmere administrative officers I was driven over to A Flight in my official squadron car, a small Hillman with a sliding roof. As we pulled up near the dispersal hut I was greeted by the sound of the Ink Spots singing 'Whispering Grass'. Their melodious voices came floating from a dilapidated old gramophone operated by a pipe-smoking, baby-faced young sergeant/pilot who bore the rather dismal title of 'Woe' Wilson. The seven pilots on duty hurriedly left the comfort of their deep old chairs and stood to attention near a pot-bellied stove, their yellow Mae Wests contrasting with the blue of their uniforms. While the Ink Spots groaned to a halt the fair-haired Umbers, A Flight's commander, showed me over the remainder of the complex.

I was disappointed with what I saw, but I knew it would be wise to hold my tongue and to attend to each matter in order of priority once I had settled in. After telling Umbers that I would require a Typhoon at 1600 hours I moved on to B Flight and found things much the same there, the only difference being that my arrival had been anticipated. An exhausted looking Harvey Sweetman was flight commander; I was glad to have his wide experience. Among his pilots were Norman Gall, a tall dark-haired boy from Rangiriri, and 'Bluey' Dall, a red-headed Australian who had joined the RNZAF while on a working holiday in New Zealand. It was just as well that the use of surnames was not permitted in the air.

While I was being introduced to the flight, two Typhoons suddenly thundered into life nearby. By the time I was out of the hut their pilots, who had been in their cockpits at instant readiness, had opened the throttles and were roaring across the grass at right angles to the main runway, downwind and in the direction of the coast. After watching them disappear into the hazy distance I instinctively picked up the nearest phone back in the dispersal hut and asked for sector control. I was told that an unidentified bogey was flying in a north-easterly direction, near Bognor, at angels one zero. Before I could say 'thanks' there came a hurried 'Sorry, sir. Bogey now identified as a friendly Hampden on fighter affiliation with the Spitfire boys of Westhampnett.' At least the Typhoon pilots were alert.

At 1600 hours I was back at A Flight and surveying the cockpit of a Typhoon, which was like looking up at a second-storey window. The small glasshouse, streamlined into the fuselage and directly behind the large engine of this seven-ton monster, was nine feet above ground. You climbed up to it by placing the toes of your shoes into small covered recesses in the metal skin. These almost invisible steps had spring-loaded covers which snapped back into position as soon as you extracted your toes. A rigger had already placed a parachute in the cockpit's metal bucket-type seat, and I lowered myself down on to it, linked up my harness, and strapped myself in securely.

I was already well familiar with the Typhoon's operating manual, and Murphy had positioned himself on the wing alongside the cockpit to give me detailed instructions on the starting up procedure. He also reminded me of some of the Typhoon's less admirable characteristics. When I felt ready I waved Murphy away, donned my helmet and oxygen mask, and plugged in my earphones. Turning the petrol cock on to the gravity position, in case of pump failure during take-off, I actuated the two toggle pumps which would shoot a mixture of oil and petrol into the cylinders and alcohol and ether into the carburettors.

The 24 cylinders of the Napier Sabre engine were forced into life by what was known as a Koffman starter, which was itself motivated by a large shotgun-type cartridge. When fired, the expansion of this charge turned over the huge motor and acted like a one-shot self-starter. If the engine did not come to life with the first explosion you could guarantee to have a fire in the air intake, which was a large aperture in the centre of the radiator scoop situated directly under the engine housing. This scoop also contained the oil and glycol radiators. A short burst from a fire extinguisher into this flaming tunnel was normally sufficient to douse the flames.

I gave the thumbs up sign to the two riggers standing by with their fire extinguishers, switched on and pressed the starter button. There was a loud noise, a cross between a hiss and bang. The engine snarled, spat, and rumbled into life. The huge propeller began to rotate, and as I eased the throttle forward the engine immediately settled into a more even and less rebellious rhythm. The two riggers put down their extinguishers and positioned themselves at either wing tip.

I rechecked the instrument panel, made sure the canopy was locked in position, and wound up my side window. Then I slowly pushed the throttle to give maximum revolutions and tested both magnetos. The Typhoon tugged, shook and roared, but there was barely a waver in the rev counter between one magneto and the other; so I eased back to less than quarter throttle, waved 'chocks away', released the brakes, and began rolling out of the bay and on to the taxiway.

The first thing I noticed was the Typhoon's poor forward visibility. Although my seat was hoisted to its maximum height I had to crab along in zigzag fashion. In a Hurricane or Spitfire you could slide your canopy back and stand up if necessary, but this was not possible in the early Typhoons. Later they were to be fitted with a bubble-type hood which not only overcame the vision problem but also gave a tremendous all-round view—the best of any aircraft I ever flew.

I called the control tower for permission to take off. The morning's wind had died away and the indicator sock by the tower was hanging like a limp rag. I braced myself and taxied straight on to the runway and applied full brake. With the control column hard back in my lap I opened up the motor to 3,000 rpm to ensure that all the plugs were cleaned off after the slow revs. The aircraft strained at the leash until

I eased back to about quarter boost. After lowering my seat and tightening my straps again, I carried out a final check of the instrument panel: oxygen five pounds—hydraulics pressure OK—flaps down 15 degrees—radiator flap open—pitch control in the 'fine' position—throttle lever screwed tight.

I let go the brakes and slowly pushed the boost lever until it reached the fully-open position. She bounded forward at a great rate and tried to swing slightly to starboard. This tendency was easily corrected by applying a little left rudder. Then we thundered down the runway as straight as an arrow before rocketing into the sky in the direction of Chichester. I flicked up the lever operating the undercarriage hydraulics and felt the wheels thud into their wing bays. She sank a little as I raised the flaps, but soon recovered when I reduced the boost and eased her propeller into a coarser pitch. Before I could check out my instrument panel again we were already over Chichester, heading fast in the direction of Selsey Bill.

My Typhoon and I began our airborne association by climbing up to 15,000 ft, where I pulled her up straight on to her tail. After reaching her zenith she spun off quickly, and I was agreeably surprised when she recovered almost as soon as I had applied corrective action. To make sure she was not fooling me I again put her into a spin, and once more she recovered beautifully. We then headed earthwards in a vertical power drive. As the speedo needle was winding up towards the 450 mph mark, I pulled her up into a loop and rolled off the top. We did ever-increasing tight turns until she blacked me out. We slow-rolled and barrel-rolled as I thrashed her about the sky for a full half hour.

She roared, screamed, groaned and whined, but apart from being rather heavy on the controls at high speeds she came through her tests with flying colours. She rocked a bit as the landing wheels were forced down into their locked positions, and she also gave a final high-pitched whine as I moved her propeller into fine pitch. Applying a few degrees of flap we swung on down into the airfield approach, levelled out above the runway, and softly eased down on to her two wheels, leaving her tail up until she dropped it of her own accord.

We were soon back in her bay by the dispersal hut, where I turned off the petrol supply cock. After a few moments she ran herself out, and with a spit, sob and weary sigh, her great three-bladed propeller came to a stop. So that was it: I was drenched in perspiration and tired out. Clambering out of the hothouse, I slid down the wing and on to the ground, thanked my fitter and rigger, and drove straight off to the officers mess.

Having my own squadron was not only an honour, it was also a great challenge, and I was determined—providing I could stay alive—to justify the trust both Air Marshal Leigh-Mallory and 'Ding' Saunders had placed in me. Furthermore, I was very conscious of the fact that mine was one of only two New Zealand Fighter squadrons in the European theatre at that time, both in 11 Group. The other was 485 Spitfire Squadron, then based at Westhampnett, a nearby airfield also under the control of the Tangmere sector.

Several New Zealand officers who had served for some years in the RAF had told me that squadrons of mixed nationalities were always the happiest, and warned that I might have problems controlling a squadron of my fellow countrymen. Apparently, six years of socialism had converted our young New Zealand men into a nation of squadron commanders. Having served only in 'mixed' squadrons, where I had seen the English and the Scottish at each other's throats over some little episode that had happened more than 300 years previously, I was naturally far from convinced.

Although some of my pilots might have thought otherwise, I do not think I approached my new command like a new broom. Instead, I set about getting to know my pilots and ground staff, a cheerful band of assorted tradesmen who were to support us ably during the long summer months ahead.

Both flight commanders, Sweetman and Umbers, were excellent and did all they could to make my settling in period easy. We held a number of squadron pep talks, during which I stipulated the need for a number of changes in the squadron routine. My ambition to have a team of fit pilots was a major issue and one of the first things we did was to appoint a sports officer. I also insisted that, regardless of the time I required their morning arrival, they must always appear for dispersal briefing freshly shaved. And every officer was to change out of battle dress and into Service uniform before attending evening mess.

Even at school I had always been a fitness fanatic. Indeed, looking back I realize I must have been one of the first joggers, and after joining the RAF I managed to squeeze my daily sweats into an already busy schedule. Strangely it was this type of activity that almost prevented me from reaching the scene of battle at all. While on my way to England with other members of my Wigram class, our

ship called in at Curaçao to refuel. She also took aboard a number
of Dutch Nazi collaborators.

These hefty arrogant individuals, locked up for most of the day,
were permitted to walk the promenade deck at certain periods in the
early morning and late afternoon. Each day, just before sunset, I
would climb into my shorts and cover myself with sweaters and my
old club rugby jersey for a mile run round the ship. One evening,
while flat out on my final lap, I was suddenly confronted by two of
these huge Dutchmen. As I went to sprint past, one hit me in the face
with his fist, catching me under the left eye and dropping me into the
scuppers. Fortunately for me two ship's officers stepped out on to the
deck at that moment, or I might well have been tossed overboard into
the shark-infested Caribbean. But my assailants had smashed my left
cheeckbone and I was forced to spend a week in my cabin bunk
nursing a mighty black eye.

Although the voyage was to last another five weeks, I never set eyes
on those two Nazi agents again. However, I had good reason to
remember them, particularly during my command of 486. I would
often suffer from severe sinus trouble, and while pulling out of a dive
during fighter bomber operations felt as if my face would explode. I
did not report my problem to my squadron doctor for fear of being
sent to hospital and perhaps losing my command. Such is the spirit
and wisdom of youth, and I suffered until the war's end when the
RAF hospital at Grantham finally took me into its care.

Apart from myself, only Harvey Sweetman had actually fought over
the Continent, and so before taking the squadron on the offensive
there was a period of training to go through in order to equip it for
the more demanding and much broader aspects of the air war.

Our first full rehearsal was rather disappointing. I took the normal
squadron of twelve into the air, flying in sections of three, but we
found this grouping cumbersome while manoeuvring into our variety
of battle stations. Three sections of four aircraft was even worse, but
the boys were quick to learn and rapidly became most proficient in
the art of formation flying.

On some days, when the Sussex skies were splashed with mighty
cumulus nimbus clouds, we would go into line astern to snake our
way among these towering giants in a catch-me-if-you-can exercise.
To go screaming into one of these giants and then suddenly rocket
up its great mountainous sides before rolling over its crest and down
the other side was unforgettable, exhilarating, and excellent training.

However, it was dangerous to misjudge your aircraft while performing this exercise. If you found you were not going to have sufficient speed and power to carry you over the top of the cloud you had to hurry and take yourself away from it.

Two years earlier in a Hurricane I had misjudged the aircraft's capacity and, as I went to roll over the top of a huge 'cunim', I literally fell into it. A cunim can be lethal and you entered one at your peril. Not only is it a great area of white turbulence, but its base will often reach the ground in heavy showers or hailstorms. Losing your horizon is bad enough, but being tossed around like a ping-pong ball in a washing machine adds even more to the discomfort. I was fortunate to be tossed out of this particular white mountain well clear of the ground. But I had received such a shaking that I flew straight and level for some time afterwards and got lost in the process.

The more I flew the Typhoon, the more convinced I became that it was essentially a low-attack aircraft. So I decided to reduce the squadron formation from twelve to eight aircraft, finding that four loose pairs were far easier to lead and manoeuvre, particularly at low levels. We proved this on our very first operation, which was intended to be a simple preview of the coast from Boulogne to the Baie de la Seine. Not expecting any air-to-air activity I took the maximum of twelve to provide as many pilots as possible with a look at our future area of operations.

We took off late in the afternoon of 8 April, and after joining up at low level in a wide sweep behind the hills around Goodwood, stuck to the tree tops until dropping over the coast near Shoreham. The sea was like glass as we slid past Brighton and Newhaven and under the white cliffs of Beachy Head, where I altered course for Boulogne. As soon as the French coast loomed into view we climbed to 3,000 ft, turned to starboard, and continued our run just out of range of the enemy coastal guns.

I had briefed the squadron to stay in fairly loose formation so that we could have a look at the coast without having to worry too much about keeping station. Instead, as we began our climb everyone closed in on me as if I were about to vanish. Le Touquet came into view, and just as I was about to tell my pilots to relax a little, two Focke Wulf 190s came at us head-on, and at our own level.

The 190s were as surprised as we were, for neither they nor we fired a shot as they passed directly over us. Then I pulled up sharply to port to find that one of them had also turned to engage. He came at me head-on with all his guns blazing. We were a little off-line and too close, yet he kept his finger on the firing button. Instinctively I ducked my head at the roar of his engine, the rattle of his cannons and the shower of his empty shell cases hitting my aircraft. I flipped over to starboard and made a dart at him as he dived for France, almost colliding with our own aircraft before I could get through to him. He left behind a thin stream of black smoke and disappeared through a spattering of light flak and into ground haze covering the Pas de Calais. The other 190 had disappeared.

The squadron was milling around in disarray as if looking for something that was not there, and I couldn't help chuckling as the boys hurriedly regrouped round me while we continued on past the Somme estuary, Le Tréport, Dieppe and Fécamp. Swinging over the Baie de la Seine we came upon a large self-propelled barge just off the moles at Le Havre. We went into an echelon to starboard and down in a fast, shallow dive, all with our four cannons blazing as we raked it from bow to stern. Flak whistled from the high ground to the west of the port, throwing up small geysers on the sea. When clear of the flak I eased back on boost control to allow any stragglers plenty of time to re-form, before setting off home to make landfall at Selsey Bill.

As we approached Tangmere I asked the squadron to close in and we passed over our airfield in tight formation before feathering out like a skein of geese and dropping noisily through the gathering dusk on to the main runway.

I had been with 486 for only a few days when the station adjutant notified me of our first casualty. Flying Officer G. G. Thomas of Auckland had been killed in a flying accident at Sutton Bridge during an air gunner refresher course. It was particularly bad news, for not only was he an experienced pilot, having recently shot down a Dornier 217 and shared in the destruction of an FW 190, he was also engaged to an attractive Tangmere WAAF nursing sister. We had not met, but he was very popular and the whole squadron spoke highly of him.

Since I was his commanding officer it was my duty to break the news to his fiancée. The information had come just before lunch and I thought it best to keep things to myself for the time being. As I tried to compose myself and decide on the best way to approach her, I might just as well have sat down to a plate of sawdust. Before leaving the dining hall I glanced across to where she was sitting, our eyes met for a fleeting moment and she smiled at me. My thoughts were scrambled as I made my way out. She followed and with a cheerful smile made straight for me as if to introduce herself. I took her hand and said I would like to see her privately. We went into a small room normally reserved for WAAF officers.

As soon as I closed the door I realized that the look on my face had already conveyed my message. I had hardly whispered 'I'm sorry' before her large blue eyes filled with tears. She seemed to anticipate every word that followed. In abject misery and despair she sank sobbing into a chair. I slipped quiety from the room, closed the door, and made my way to the solitude of my own quarters.

Once we had cut our Typhoon squadron formations down to eight aircraft, although we may not have qualified for a prewar Hendon air display, I don't think any squadron in the RAF could have outshone us in the art of formation flying and all-round manoeuvrability. The New Zealand pilots would cling to me like leeches, whether I was upside down, on my nose, or standing on my tail. We did a number of offensive missions, mainly escorting Bombphoons— a Typhoon loaded with bombs—which was good experience for many of the new pilots.

However, it was not until the morning of 14 April that I had the opportunity of firing my cannons again. Group Captain McGregor, who was about to relinquish command of the station, phoned from the sector operations room to report enemy plots on the board, midway between Cherbourg Peninsula and Le Havre. They were flying low and appeared to be escorting a surface vessel of some sort, since the plots were moving slowly across the board.

I took Pilot Officer R. Fitzgibbon, a Culverden boy, as my number two, and invited Harvey Sweetman to come along with one of his B Flight pilots. We hurried off across a glass-like sea, and as we approached the general area of our search we came upon patches of heavy sea mist and began a square search. After about five minutes we flew directly over what appeared to be an E-boat. Pulling up sharply over its deck, and expecting a shower of flak, I caught a quick glimpse of some of its crew, who looked as surprised as I felt. The mist, which was really more of a thick haze, was only about 200 ft deep, and as I broke into the clear sky above it, I came almost directly under and behind a pair of Me 109s in wide search formation.

My zoom-up from below closed me in so rapidly to the 109 nearest me that I had to open fire almost immediately. I got in quite a decent burst and bits flew off him in all directions, including what appeared to be his canopy, which flashed past my own cockpit by inches. I was forced to pull quickly away to starboard, otherwise my propeller would have minced off his tail and we would both have been in a similar predicament.

I could see he was in real trouble. His propeller began to windmill and short sharp bursts of black and white smoke began leaving his exhausts; but I could see no fire. I looked around for Sweetman. He had apparently followed the other 109 down into the haze as it fled quickly for France. Fitz was still with me and had taken a shot at our 109 directly after I had pulled out to the starboard.

As our victim dropped his nose into a slow shallow dive towards the sea, I throttled back in formation with him. He was trying to climb out of his cockpit and I could see quite clearly the terrified expression on his round young face. You do things when your blood is up and your heart is pounding that you would not do under normal circumstances. I followed him down in the direction of a reasonably clear patch of sea, where I thought he was going to attempt a ditching, but he must have changed his mind, or was perhaps injured. Still clinging to the side of his cockpit, he pulled himself out on to the starboard wing when only about 100 ft above the water. For reasons which I have never been able to analyse, I pressed the firing button again, and he and his aircraft hit the sea almost simultaneously in a fountain of spray, framed only by the pattern of my own cannon fire.

As Fitz came alongside me while I was turning for home, he gave me the thumbs up sign. I buried my head in the cockpit and was suddenly overcome with a feeling of deep remorse. When you shoot down an aircraft, you don't normally think of its pilot. But in this case we had come face to face, the victor and the vanquished. Why had I fired that last burst? It had not been necessary. I tried to console myself in the fact that he was the author of his own destruction, and had been far too low to bale out. Yet why could I not have kept my bloody fingers out of his final moment? The passing years have not erased the magnitude of this brief encounter. I often see him looking back at me—and well may he ask 'Who won?'

It did not take long to discover that the human material I had in 486 was very much above average. Although the pilots were from all walks of life, most were from the smaller towns and the country districts of New Zealand. They all had that quiet, rugged politeness that stems from the closeness of small communities. I could picture their mothers baking cakes for the church fairs and their local

Plunket Society. I could see their fathers helping out the neighbours with the sheep shearing.

It would be unfair if I attempted to sort out even one boy for special mention for his prowess in the air. Once we got to understand one another I don't think there was a single pilot who would not have followed me willingly into the jaws of hell. In fact during the months of low-attack missions that followed, many of them did.

3

Squadron Life

On the morning of 16 April I came close to getting shot down. Crowley-Milling had a squadron of Bombphoons at Lasham. We arranged to meet him over the south coast near Shoreham and escort his squadron on an early-morning raid on Tricqueville, an enemy airfield near Caen. The idea was to stay low over the sea in order to keep below the enemy's radar screen until approaching Fécamp, where we would climb to 6,000 ft. On crossing the French coast we would proceed in an almost straight line behind Le Havre and across the Seine to our target in Normandy.

I don't know why 'Crow' chose this approach. I would have preferred a much shorter run-in to the target by way of the Baie de la Seine, and a coastal crossing in the region of Ouistreham or Deauville. It could have have given us the valuable element of surprise. But since we were only the escort it was not my job to argue or tell him what to do.

All went according to plan. By the time we were over our target, a number of FW 190s had already taken off, and as the Bombphoons whistled down and unloaded, I could see bombs bursting among other aircraft in the act of getting airborne. I was sorely tempted to go down, but knew this could be fatal for both us and our charges because we could be suddenly bounced from above.

'Crow' got his boys back up quickly and was soon in formation again, so we made up two relatively compact fighting units. However, we had agreed the night before that as soon as his mission was completed, he would return on the reciprocal course to our outward leg, leaving me to lead my squadron down into the Seine estuary in the hope of sighting enemy E-boats.

Once the Bombphoons were safely across the Seine, I put my nose down and the squadron followed me in a steep dive to within a few feet of the water. The E-boats must have returned from their nightly activities earlier than usual and were all safely tucked away out of sight. So after waggling my wings at some small French fishing boats on their way to sea, we pressed on in the direction of Le Havre. Several huge oil storage tanks on the southern perimeter of the port came into view, and we went straight at them with our cannon fire. Our shells exploded like a firework display against the sides of these ugly monsters and smoke began to rise.

As I turned slightly to port, I noticed some shipping just in the roadstead, not far from the moles that guarded the harbour entrance. I pulled up to about 500 ft, then put down my nose again, and with guns blazing made straight for the nearest flak ship. A great wall of orange and red tracer, studded with black puffs of heavier flak, came racing up to meet me. It was like flying through the jets of a coloured fountain. As I pulled up over the ship's superstructure I felt several thuds and my aircraft shuddered and began rolling to starboard with her nose pointing towards the heavens. I caught a quick glimpse of Murphy behind and below me, but I was far too busy to see what was happening to the rest of the squadron.

My aircraft completed several rolls. I jammed my right arm between the side of the cockpit and the control column and with both hands straining managed to stop her revolving round her longitudinal axis, and hold her on a more or less even keel. I kept the engine at full blast to take me as far as possible from the enemy coast in case I had to bale out.

Looking up at the rear vision mirror to see how the rest of my boys were faring, I was just in time to see an aircraft at the tail end of our gaggle hit the sea in a fountain of spray. It took the anxiety out of my own predicament, and I tried to count how many were still behind me. Twice I counted six, but it was like trying to tally a flight of starlings. At one stage I totalled nine.

We were well clear of the French coast and had pulled up to about 2,000 ft before I eased back on the throttle. I was thankful to find the pressure on my right arm had eased considerably. I was able to look around and counted all seven aircraft. I was far from certain but with my own that made the full eight. My left hand was now relatively free and I was able to call each aircraft in turn, but there was no reply from Red 2, Flying Officer Norman Gall, and my heart sank again. Had one of 'Crow's' boys joined us or was I just seeing things?

The green fields of Sussex looked even sweeter than usual as we crossed in over the coast. I instructed the squadron to go ahead and land. I would follow. As they passed me I counted again, and my spirits rose; all our aircraft bore the same squadron letters. They soon dropped away in the direction of Tangmere leaving me in the empty sky to sort out my own landing problems. I did a wide half-circuit and made a long steady approach. Slowing down on my run in to the main runway, the pressure came off my arms and I was able to ease her down without further trouble.

As the crash tender and ambulance returned to their places by the watch office, I slowly taxied over the grass towards A Flight dispersal, drenched in sweat and absolutely exhausted. Thanking God that I was home again, I jumped down from the aircraft, sank my face into the grass, and breathed deeply the sweet smell of friendly earth. After a few moments I opened my eyes. Right in front of my nose a colony of tiny black ants was carrying out its daily chores as if nothing had ever happened. Some rude sergeant pilot cycling past on the taxiway did not recognize me in my prone position and called out: 'Looking for a four-leaf clover?'

It didn't take the engineering officer long to sort out the damage, but he could hardly understand how the aircraft had ever flown home. I had taken what appeared to be two 37 mm shells in my starboard aileron. One had completely locked the internal mechanism; the other had forced up a large flap of metal on the trailing edge. The resistance of the air flow over this, combined with the locked mechanism, had made me fight hard to continue flying.

The best news was of Norman Gall of B Flight, who had not answered my call. An Me 109 had swooped down on his tail and misjudged his distance when just above the water. He had hit Gall's slipstream, dropped a wing tip, touched the sea, and cartwheeled in a fountain of spray into a thousand pieces. Seconds before killing himself he had blown Gall's wireless set to pieces and buckled the armour plating just behind his head. So I guess in some ways Red 2 was even luckier than his leader.

Physical fitness was to be a prominent feature of our station life, and the first organized sport we played was a game of hockey against a team of WAAFs from the sector operations room. It did not matter whether any of my pilots had ever held a hockey stick in their hands before, or whether the opposition was male or female. Exercise was the primary objective. So one misty afternoon we gathered down at

Bishop Otter College where the WAAFs were billeted, and used their huge gymnasium for changing into our sports gear.

A new padre had arrived at Tangmere a few weeks previously, and had taken a liking to my New Zealand boys. He would spend hours in the bar listening to their chatter while drinking endless glasses of lemonade. He always gave me the impression that if he had his time over again he would rather be a pilot than a clergyman. He had asked if he could join us for our afternoon sport and he arrived in at the gymnasium clad in a pair of khaki shorts reaching below his knees, short black socks and white sandshoes.

Out in the middle of the gym floor stood a huge medicine ball weighing all of 40 lbs. Our padre must have thought it was a balloon. Full of *joi de vivre*, he pranced across the floor and took a mighty kick at it. From where I was standing on the far side of the gym, the sound of his foot breaking was like a pistol shot. The padre raised his face to the heavens, hopped around on one leg, and loudly and repeatedly broke the second commandment. Soon he was taken away to sick quarters where his foot was encased in plaster.

Needless to say the WAAFs, who were experts, won the game by a wide margin, and almost neutered me while doing so. A sturdily-built lass from Somerset had let drive with a hefty swing at goal. The ball failed to pass between my legs by an inch or two. I dropped to the grass in wide-eyed agony and had to be helped off the scene of battle.

I do not believe I was the kind of officer who went round looking for faults in subordinates. Having worked my way up through the ranks, I was perhaps more qualified than some to appreciate the wide gap that often existed between the rank and file and the self-styled service elite. However, if you are trained to fight until your blood runs hot, I suppose it is only natural that you should eventually find enemies on both sides of the fence.

Every member of the RAF was a small cog in a large wheel, but some officers—fortunately not many—thought their status entitled them to believe otherwise. This applied mainly to the administrative side of the service, although I believe it also existed in the flying side of Training Command. I had outlived many pilots in my three years of operations, and I may have been a little biased or over-protective of my air crew.

However, as far as I was concerned every RAF establishment existed for one purpose only, to support those who flew. Of course

we couldn't do without our maintenance staff or all other levels of
the administration. But it was the air crew alone who were asked to
face the dangerous skies.

It was with the medical administration at Tangmere that I first
found reason to differ. Every squadron had its own doctor, normally
a flying officer or flight-lieutenant—ranks which were poor com-
pensation for their long years of study and in relation to their civilian
status. But that was not my argument. I was adamant that our doctor
should attend all briefings, whatever the hour or nature of our
missions. However, without my authority our doctor had been included in the station routine roster, and instead of holding a watching
brief over my own personnel when it mattered most, he could well
be at station sick quarters attending to a boil on the backside of a
cook or clerk.

Squadron briefing and debriefing were the times when a doctor
could help his commanding officer to sort out those boys who were
beginning to feel the strain. At 23 years of age, being neither a doctor
nor a qualified psychologist, I was at a disadvantage without him.
And it was unfair on my pilots. In most cases I could pick the telltale
signs of the man who was losing confidence in himself. He would
fidget through the briefing and smoke innumerable cigarettes, often
stubbing them out soon after they were lit. He would spend far too
much time in the loo. On returning from his combat mission he would
have too much to say, and generally in a rapid falsetto.

One young pilot officer had sat in the mess reading a copy of the
Tatler. This was quite normal—but not with the magazine upside
down. He was not one of my own squadron and I had never spoken
to him before. I took my after-lunch coffee over to where he sat, to
make sure it was not just the cover that was the wrong way up. The
magazine was indeed upside down and the pilot officer was obviously
still far away over France, for every now and then his feet gave a little
twitch.

I quietly placed my hand upon his shoulder and asked him if he
would mind giving me the correct time. He came back to earth and
his wide open face seemed to convey a message of distress, although
I think he was pleased that I should have noticed him. I could see by
the pinkish colour of his eyes and their contracted pupils that he was
troubled and badly in need of a change of occupation.

I passed on my observations to his commanding officer, but he
appeared to be uninterested and even seemed to resent my intrusion.
Two days later the boy was shot down, posted as missing believed

killed. I often think that he might be alive today if his CO had been a little more perceptive and helped him through his crisis.

It may seem strange, but I encouraged my pilots to drink. A few tankards of mild-and-bitter acted as a safety valve, and the boys could unwind by letting off as much steam as they wished. But the boys seldom drank to excess, and if anyone abused my trust I would immediately ground him for 48 hours. The mess bar was a good place for the squadron doctor, too, for a normally reticent pilot would often open up and bring to the surface some of the problems that he would otherwise have kept hidden. There would be more Huns shot down from the smoky atmosphere of the mess bar than would ever fall from the flak-torn skies over France.

When a new station commander, Group Captain W. J. (Paddy) Crisham, arrived at Tangmere, my battle with the station medical administration came to a sudden and happy conclusion. I had first met Paddy at Fighter Command HQ, which he visited soon after recovering from a night crash which had smashed his face and nearly cost him his life. Paddy's soft brogue and unassuming manner were unique among officers of his rank and long service. His arrival was like a breath of fresh Irish mountain air and he became a father figure to all of us. Under his new orders our squadron doctor became a permanent asset at every briefing. So, too, was Paddy, no matter how dark or cold the dawn.

The space between the main perimeter taxiway and our dispersal huts, a strip of ground about 30 × 6 yds, was often a sea of mud. I was flying off to Troon in Scotland to lecture to a combined operations course for a day or two, and informed my pilots that I wanted to see a big improvement in this untidy piece of ground when I returned. On arriving back at Tangmere I could hardly believe my eyes. They had not only cleaned up the area, but had set out lawns, white pebble paths and ornamental gardens already planted with asters, marigolds and small shrubs. The lawns had been laid in square blocks of turf. I knew this had not been found on the station, but since no one seemed willing to tell me, I did not enquire too closely. The mystery was solved some days later when an irate farmer complained that my boys had 'borrowed' the turf from him.

The whole place was like a new pin. Even the dispersal floor lino had been polished until it shone like a mirror, and several pieces of new furniture had replaced the old threadbare, springless armchairs. Behind the dispersal huts the ground staff had also been busy. They had set-to with spades and rakes and established a sizeable vegetable garden. I thanked the men collectively and that evening we all took off on a pub crawl round the Sussex countryside.

As the volume of our offensive mounted, so did the interest of the Press, and a number of Air Ministry bulletins featuring our activities appeared in the daily papers. This appeared to be a signal for some of the New Zealand 'chairborne' division at Halifax House in London to muscle in on our emergence from obscurity, and they suddenly started to invite themselves down to Tangmere.

Now although we were designated as a New Zealand squadron, we were in fact under the jurisdiction of the RAF, and the only claim the New Zealand Air Force could have on us was that our pilots were New Zealanders, as were some of the wireless mechanics. The ground staff were predominantly RAF and in some of the so-called New Zealand squadrons a number of the air crew, including their commanding officers, were English.

I was determined to put a stop to these open visits forthwith. Writing to Halifax House, I requested that in future any staff wishing to visit my squadron must first apply in writing, stating the nature of their visit and the reason for it. I was not trying to be difficult, but some of these people were annoying my boys. Needless to say, the visits stopped, but there was one gentleman who arrived needing no invitation. He came at short notice on 17 April 1943, and was accompanied by our AOC, Air Marshal 'Ding' Saunders. He was our diminutive Minister of Defence, The Honourable Fred Jones, the Labour MP for Dunedin Central.

Many of our pilots were farmers and staunch Conservatives, and thus the Minister's welcome was somewhat tepid. He looked a comic figure, dressed in crumpled black suit, narrow trousers (in mourning at half-mast) and lace-up boots. He displayed an almost childlike desire to sit in my Typhoon, which stood directly outside the dispersal door. So we hoisted him up on to the wing of the aircraft and helped him into the cockpit, where he almost disappeared from sight. I spent ten minutes explaining the layout and function of the many instruments, and warned him to be careful of the undercarriage lever which, if released, would immediately set my aircraft on its belly. Then I let myself down to the ground so that he could play about to his heart's content.

My pilots were dutifully looking towards the open cockpit when the Minister's small head appeared over the side. In a voice full of amazed wonder he called out: 'So this is a Spitfire. How many engines has it got?'

In the cool quiet hours of the morning we would lower ourselves into our cockpits, and before the first flush of sunrise appeared in the eastern sky, the roar of our low-flying formation would shatter the tranquillity of the Sussex countryside. The dark lines of hedgerows, and the lighter wisps of cottage smoke, would slip beneath us as we hurried off towards the Channel and the lairs of our German enemy. You could almost smell the sweet morning breath of the English countryside. It was hard to believe one might be setting out on one's final flight.

As we dropped over the beaches and flew low over the flatness of the Channel, sea birds would rise off the surface and whip past in scattered wild array. We had to avoid them; with a Typhoon cruising at 300 mph a bird could hit the leading edge of your wing like a piece of shrapnel and bury itself in the metal right back into the main spar. One of our pilots stopped one in the air intake in the centre of the radiator scoop immediately beneath the motor. It choked the engine and he was forced to make a crash-landing.

In our early-morning visits to the French coast our prime purpose was to intercept the E-boat flotillas returning from their night raids before they reached the safety of their home ports. They generally travelled in groups of a dozen or more and were escorted, once they were back in the Baie de La Seine, by flakships, which remained with them until they were safely tucked away for the day.

In my earlier days I had carried out many shipping strikes while flying Hurricanes, and had learned from experience that it did not pay to approach the target directly unless favoured by poor visibility, when you might be lucky enough to surprise their gunners. Later, when leading my own formations, I would approach the convoy and fly round it, just out of range of its flak.

Most gunners were obviously of the opinion that the best method of defence is attack, and every gun would open up at the same time in the hope that the great volume of multicoloured tracer would frighten us away. Most of the lighter weapons were fed by drums and belts, and I would notice a sudden falling off in density while they were being changed and replenished. The heavier flak would continue bursting, but this never worried me so much as the quadruple pom-poms, or 'Chicago pianos' as we called them. As soon as this lull occurred I would peel off down, and then it was every man for himself. With thumbs held firmly on our firing buttons we would rake the vessel we had chosen from stem to stern, or vice versa, depending on which way we had decided to break away.

The worst part in these attacks was in the recovery. As you zoomed up over the vessel, you felt rather vulnerable behind, and had to weave away from it as best you could. The times when I collected a packet were nearly always when I was pulling out of an attack and I nearly had my tail blown off on more than one occasion.

To add to the variety of our operations we also carried out our standing Channel patrols, and in early May we escorted Bostons and Bombphoons on several bombing raids against enemy airfields, mainly Caen, Poix and Abbeville. On 4 May we had a decent sort of strike against two coasters escorted by a couple of flakships in the roadstead at Le Havre. And on 13 May we escorted some bombers to Abbeville, where we had the satisfaction of seeing many bombs bursting in an area of the airfield heavily infested with German aircraft.

On the early morning of 16 May we suffered a sad blow when, without even firing a shot, we lost Flying Officer Brown. We had just left the Cherbourg peninsula and were making our way at sea level to Le Havre via Ouistreham when we ran into a flotilla of 15 E-boats, escorted by a number of flakships. While we stood off to allow their guns to run down, Brown radioed that he was in trouble. I do not think he could have been hit by flak, for we were at extreme range. He may have had engine failure or he may have run into a geyser. If this had happened the motor would snuff out immediately. Whatever the trouble, he had managed to make enough height to bale out.

For his sake I left the flotilla alone and we hung around until we saw an escort vessel approach his dinghy. After arriving back at Tangmere, an international distress signal was sent out to the enemy to make sure he was picked up. The normal custom was to acknowledge such a signal, but this time there was no acknowledgment, so a special war of attrition began between myself and the E-boats and flakships in the Baie de La Seine.

On 17 May we escorted Bombphoons to Coxyde airfield in the Pas de Calais and although we ran into some intense and heavy flak, no enemy fighters were engaged. However, the next day was to be disastrous. I was asked by Squadron Leader Leo De Soomer, a Belgian in command of No 3 Squadron, if I would escort his squadron on a dawn raid on Poix airfield. I was delighted to accept. Poix and Caen Carpiquet were the two hottest spots on the Continent as far as I was concerned, but also No 3 Squadron was the first I had served in. We flew into West Malling to stay the night and hold a joint squadron briefing.

De Soomer was a delightful person, but I believe this was to be his first Bombphoon mission. At the briefing I said my piece and it was agreed that the Bombphoons should return home at 6,000 ft as quickly as possible after releasing their bombs. We would return as two squadrons and in battle formation, i.e. as loose pairs. No 1 Squadron was to act as withdrawal cover and pick us up between Poix and the Somme estuary.

For reasons best known to himself, De Soomer changed his mind. Without telling me he rebriefed his pilots the next morning just before take-off, asking them to return from Poix at nought feet, or ground level. Had I been aware of this I most certainly would have queried this change of plan.

On our way in, as we were approaching Poix, I was warned by Blue 1 that a number of enemy aircraft were up-sun, but I could not see them myself and in close support we pressed on towards our target, a little above and to port of the Bombphoons. Flak came belting up as De Soomer peeled off and led his squadron in line astern down on to his target. I did a sweep around and waited for them to come up and reform, but their briefing order did not materialize and I was mystified as to what was happening. With enemy aircraft above us, and No 1 Squadron somewhere in the vicinity below us, I didn't dare go down. It looked as if some of No 3 Squadron were actually flying inland as tracer began following aircraft that seemed to be heading in the direction of Amiens. Two aircraft exploded on the ground to the east of Poix.

As we left the target area two more aircraft crashed and exploded to the west of the target, but I could not see whether they were friend or foe. I took my squadron out at the agreed height of 6,000 ft and sighted none of our Bombphoons until we were over the Somme estuary. Five had been shot down by flak or fighters, and No 1 Squadron did not put in an appearance at all.

As soon as we landed I phoned 'Ding' Saunders at 11 Group and asked for an immediate enquiry. Then both Leo De Soomer and I set off for Uxbridge to discuss the reasons for this disaster. De Soomer did not try to shelve the blame; he simply said he had changed his mind about the target briefing that morning—very much to his sorrow. Even if No 1 Squadron had put in an appearance, I do not think it would have made any difference to the overall result. It was a cruel, sharp lesson for No 3 Squadron, and for me too, and in future I made sure that all briefings were strictly followed.

I had to wait until 25 May before I downed another enemy aircraft. Several sneak raiders were getting in and away again in the Brighton area, and I thought I would take a look at Friston, a small grass airfield on top of the chalk cliffs near Newhaven, a few miles east of Brighton. I took Flying Officer Alan Smith and Flight-Lieutenant Umbers with me, with the idea of inspecting the facilities and basing a flight there during daylight hours.

We had no sooner landed and left our cockpits when a red Very light shot up from the control tower. Realizing there was something doing, we scrambled back into our cockpits, started up, switched into the Kenley frequency, and roared off over the cliffs, turning starboard towards Brighton. As the bombs were already exploding, I knew it would be too late if we continued on to Brighton or Hove, so I veered to port and out to sea in the hope of intercepting the raiders in their line of flight for the French coast. I sighted a gaggle of about a dozen, well out to sea and close to the water, and we swung in behind.

Then two stragglers suddenly appeared to starboard—an FW 190 and an Me 109. Both had obviously stayed to beat up the streets of Brighton and were well behind the main raiders. I instructed Umbers and Smith to take the 109 to the right while I set about the FW 190, which was by this time almost dead ahead of me. My first burst made him weave, and slowed him up considerably. I held my fire until I was much closer, and gave him a long burst. Cannon shells exploded all over him and I was about to press the button again, when his port wing hit the water and he cartwheeled and disintegrated in a ball of spray, black smoke and fire. Pieces of flying metal from his plane struck the leading edge of both my wings, and hit my armour-plated glass windscreen. I took some cine film of what remained of my victim—a small column of smoke and a few bits and pieces floating on the water.

While Umbers was firing at his 109, four of my boys arrived on the scene from Tangmere, mistook him for an FW 190, and scored several hits from behind with cannon fire. It was one of the perils of working with mixed freqencies and we were forced to break off the engagement. But we soon sorted ourselves out, and arrived back at Tangmere feeling both pleased and disappointed.

I tore a strip off one of the young pilots who had attacked Umbers, and felt rather sorry for him when I saw him trying to fight back tears. But I had to make him aware of the dangers that lurked in the skies, even when we were on top of the enemy. He did not live long enough to heed my plea. A few days later he was shot down by flak and disappeared into the sea off Le Havre.

'Smile, and the Lord Smiles With You.' The small steel mirror above the washbasin in my room was still shining out its heavenly prayer. But I was finding it increasingly harder to respond. I had the feeling that the twilight at the end of each day marked the end of another passing year.

We wound up May by leading two squadrons of Bombphoons on the steelworks at Caen. The German defences were very active with flak, and they hit several of our aircraft, including my own, but we did not meet up with any enemy fighters. I had several new boys on this mission, and could see by the way they were 'see-sawing' at their throttles that they were more than a little anxious. As calmly as I could among the bursting flak, I asked them to settle down and told them there was nothing to worry about. They improved but still seemed to want to compete with me for the lead.

The Bombphoons dropped their bombs on the steel works, and we swept on over Caen Carpiquet airfield. There the Germans greeted us with an even heavier concentration of flak. I saw some of my tail-enders try to weave their way through it, hoping to avoid this network of fire, but this was useless. To calm them down I did three slow rolls in succession. This had the desired effect and they settled down like old stagers. We crossed easily through a final flak reception midway between Arromanches and Courseulles.

During June we did a number of sweeps, all to a similar pattern, then on 24 June I fought with two FW 190s—one a friend and one a foe! I do not know on whose authority the friendly FW 190 came down to Tangmere, but I believe it was from the Central Fighter Establishment at Farnborough, where they tested all captured enemy aircraft. It was wearing the RAF battledress and roundels, and was flown by a competent RAF pilot.

I engaged in mock combat with the 190 in the skies above Sussex and was surprised by its speed and manoeuvrability. But I was confident I could get the better of it, providing we remained below 10,000 ft. Above that altitude it was a different story. The higher we went the more like a carthorse I became. However, since we were essentially on low-attack operations, our chances of becoming embarrassed at 10,000 ft or above were fairly remote.

That afternoon I encountered another FW 190, only this time it was not a game. We had escorted Bombphoons to Abbeville again, and on our way out to the coast a small number of FW 190s kept niggling at our tails, without coming in close enough to mix it with us. The Bombphoons put their noses down as we crossed out near Cayeux, and we followed suit. So did the enemy. As far as I could see, they were not closing on us and I thought I would hold our course until we were clear of the coast. While I was keeping my eye on the enemy behind, two FW 190s suddenly jumped us from nowhere, and I quickly broke to starboard.

The FW 190s foolishly dived under us towards the sea, and this gave us the immediate advantage. I took a quick look round while sprinting down after them. Fitz, my No 2, was hanging on to my tail, and I could see nothing else close to me except our own Typhoons. Within seconds I was firing directly down on an FW 190. He turned to port close to the water. My deflection was astray—I could see cannon shells splashing in the sea a few feet behind his tail. Suddenly we were at the same level and locked in a desperate battle to out-turn each other.

I applied the pressure to get my sights ahead of him, but I kept losing my vision as the blood was forced away from my head; a little less pressure on the control column would bring my sight back into focus. I could see him looking back at me on the other side of our tight circle. I knew he was experiencing the same effects, and although I could feel my own aircraft staggering a little, I continued to apply the pressure. I was beginning to gain on him, but was still well off the required amount of deflection. With my heart pounding in my throat, I applied some top rudder to get above him. Just as I did so, his wings gave a wobble and he flicked over and hit the sea upside down.

I saw the great shower of spray his aircraft sent up, but not much else. I blacked out, went out of control myself, and recovered from my downward plunge just clear of the water. According to Fitz I had spun upwards. It could easily have been the other way, and both my Luftwaffe opponent and I would have finished up under water.

Flight-Lieutenant Umbers had also knocked down a FW 190, so it proved an exciting and successful day. Nevertheless, as we made off home towards Dungeness I looked down at my hands and saw

that my fingers were trembling. And I could feel perspiration trick-
ling down the backs of my legs.

The Typhoon's cockpit was a real sweat box at the best of times. It
possessed no air vents and was overheated by the massive 24-cylinder
engine. There was always danger from carbon monoxide poison, and
we had to use oxygen at all times. With our canopies closed we were
almost hermetically sealed in. During the summer months the heat
became almost unbearable, particularly since we were flying so close
to the ground on most of our operations.

I took the matter up with the Air Ministry, but their boffin boys
fluffed around for so long that I finally asked for an immediate
enquiry. When two Air Ministry staff arrived at Tangmere we were
away over France, so they waited for us in our dispersal huts. Fortunately it was a warm day, and when we got back I took off my
singlet in front of them and wrung it out, forming a large pool of
water on the floor. Some of my other pilots wrung out their singlets,
and a miniature lake was being created on the dispersal hut floor. The
two visitors left convinced that there was a problem, but still mutter-
ing about monoxide poisoning. I bade them goodbye and demanded
action within seven days.

There was none. So instead my engineering officer and I devised
a simple solution. He drilled a half-inch hole in the leading edge of
the port wing, just to starboard of the No 2 cannon. We fixed up a
rubber hose to lead from this through the wing and into the cockpit,
where it was connected to a manually-operated valve fitted just to the
left of the instrument panel. The movement of the aircraft shot a
stream of cold air into our cockpits, and by manipulating the valve
we could achieve a reasonable level of comfort. It was an inelegant
solution, but would the boffins agree to it? Not at all! It had to be
done their way. They insisted that the entry hole should be positioned
in front of our windscreen, and all subsequent aircraft off the
assembly line were fitted with this arrangement. I am still convinced
that our idea was better and safer.

As we moved into July and the hot summer days, the weight of our
commitment became even heavier. We would often be in the Baie de
La Seine at 5 o'clock in the morning, landing back at Tangmere after
our last operation just as the dusk was fading into night. One evening,
setting off in the direction of Le Havre, we encountered one of the
most beautiful sights I have ever experienced. We were after E-boats,

and flying just above the surface of a glass-like sea. There was not a cloud in sight, nor a wisp of wind. Then halfway between the Isle of Wight and Cap d'Antifer, a massive cumulus nimbus cloud loomed into view that must have reached from ground level to upwards of 20,000 ft. Drawing closer I could see it covered Le Havre and most of the Seine estuary. While the sun sank behind us this immense snow-white cloud began to blush and by the time we were in the bay it had turned deep crimson. The sea reflected this gigantic pillar of fire, our Typhoons were red, and even the sea birds flashed by like showers of glowing embers. For a few minutes it left me almost breathless.

As we cruised by in the direction of Deauville, the cloud began to lose its brilliant colour. By the time we had turned for home, although it was still capped in pink, its lower reaches had changed to an ominous grey, reminding me of the great areas of danger that lay directly beneath it. It was nearly dark when we landed, eight pilots without a word to say. As I closed the dispersal door, they had already melted into the silence of the night.

Amongst frequent visitors to 486 Squadron dispersal was Anthony Eden, the Foreign Secretary, who was to become Prime Minister in 1955. He had a country home called Biddington, near Chichester, a few miles east of Tangmere, and I believe he became genuinely fond of the New Zealand boys. Whenever he visited the station, he seemed to spend most of his time with them. One morning I was told by Paddy Crisham, our station commander, that Mr Eden would be calling in at the squadron dispersal, accompanied by his wife Beatrice—and were due in twenty minutes!

The dispersal walls were liberally adorned with pinups. So we hastily obliterated them with maps of France and Holland and had the girls reasonably obscured by the time our visitors arrived. In the centre of the room stood a glass tank containing some goldfish we had 'borrowed' from the pond in the grounds of a nearby hospital. The goldfish proved a good talking point at first, but then Mrs Eden showed more interest in something on the wall, near to our pot-bellied stove. The heat had warped a map, and a bare leg was showing below the Brest peninsula. Mrs Eden lifted the map in the region of St Nazaire, uncovering a nude blonde reclining on a polar bear skin. A copy of the poem 'Eskimo Nell' was also attached. Mrs Eden, displaying even greater interest, drifted from one wall to another, and by the time she had inspected all four—and appeared to be looking for a fifth—most of my brave New Zealand boys had drifted away.

This embarrassing interlude was suddenly interrupted by a phone call from Sector Operations. A reconnaissance plane had sighted several E-boats and I was requested to scramble my squadron off to the Baie de La Seine. Minutes later we were tucking up our wheels and roaring off in the direction of Le Havre. I set my pitch control for cruising revs, and wondered how many of my pilots had taken off without their maps. However, the E-boats had apparently beaten us into one of the smaller French ports, for the bay was clear of shipping apart from a few fishing boats whose crews gave us a friendly wave.

By the time we returned the Edens had left. Although I saw the Foreign Secretary from time to time, I did not see Mrs Eden again until well into the summer when one beautiful Sunday morning Paddy Crisham phoned to say we were both invited to Biddington for tennis that afternoon. I had not touched a racquet since leaving grammar school, and of all ball games tennis was my weakest. I also had a squadron sweep laid on over France which would occupy most of my morning. But Paddy would listen to no excuses: his car would pick me up at the officers' mess at 1 p.m. sharp.

I hurriedly phoned my batwoman, and told her to see that a fresh change of clothes, including my other pair of underpants, was laid out ready on my bed. Much to my subsequent regret, I also gave her the afternoon off.

The squadron sweep accomplished, we landed back at Tangmere, our clothes soaked with sweat as usual. I dived under a cool shower, rushed a sandwich, and began climbing into my freshly laundered underwear. But it did not take me long to discover that my spare underpants had only one button instead of the usual two, the survivor hanging on by a couple of threads. Unfortunately my batwoman had already taken off, and I frantically hunted round—unsuccessfully— for a safety pin.

By almost 1 p.m. I had scrambled into a borrowed pair of oversized cream flannels and rushed down the stairs to Paddy's waiting car. A short drive brought us to Biddington where Mr and Mrs Eden were charming hosts, but their impeccable attire and air of supreme elegance did little to boost my morale.

It was agreed that I should partner Mrs Eden and Paddy Mr Eden. As soon as it became obvious that none of us was a candidate for Wimbledon, my confidence began to rise and all went smoothly until it was my turn to serve. Then, as I rose up on my toes, I felt something snap, and a small white button lay at my feet.

You can serve reasonably well with your legs crossed, but moving about the court is much more difficult. As my underpants slowly descended into the crutch of my flannels I turned the colour of a well-boiled lobster and my feet became glued to the court. Our hostess, correctly sensing that my mind was elsewhere, asked with great concern: 'Are you feeling all right, Scottie?'

Clutching the large bulge in the seat of my flannels with one hand I replied that I had just had an accident. With an air that seemed to suggest it was an everyday event, she graciously answered: 'Don't worry, Scottie, it happens in all sorts of company. I'll show you the way to the bathroom.' Hastily I stammered that I thought my problem could be rectified by taking refuge for a moment behind a massive oak tree, which stood alongside the court. At this her eyes opened wide, and with unseemly haste I turned and inched my way towards the trunk of the friendly old oak.

Once behind the tree I found that I was able to restore some sort of temporary order and, emerging sheepishly and still lobster coloured, the game continued. Needless to say, my play did not improve—but then neither did my partner's.

Before I left Tangmere to command RAF Station Hawkinge, further up the coast and above the cliffs of Dover, I asked Mr Eden if he would consider accepting the honorary rank of Air Commodore to 486 (New Zealand) Squadron. Winston Churchill was already filling a similar position in 615 (County of Surrey) Squadron. Mr Eden was delighted, and I wasted no time in setting the wheels in motion by contacting Bill (later Sir William) Jordan, our High Commissioner in London. He was most enthusiastic and suggested I put my proposition on paper and send it to Halifax House. I was duly notified that Wellington had been advised, and there the matter had to rest as far as I was concerned. However, I felt sure New Zealand would honour both Britain's Foreign Secretary and 486 Squadron by agreeing to my proposal.

Many weeks later I was invited to lunch at the Jordans', where in the course of our conversation I introduced the subject of Mr Eden's honorary Air Commodoreship. I was shattered when Bill told me that Prime Minister Peter Fraser had thought my proposition impertinent. He had stated that no New Zealand squadron would have a Tory Air Commodore as long as he was Labour Prime Minister.

Bill Jordan was visibly upset. Born at Ramsgate, the son of a fisherman, he had served as a constable in London's Metropolitan Police before emigrating to New Zealand. A Privy Councillor, he was the most loved of all our High Commissioners and reckoned he was one of the few men who could put PC both before and after his name. Bill had been wounded during service in the First World War and was in London during the blitz. He felt that Mr Fraser's attitude was as much an insult to him as to the boys of 486. I also found it particularly hard to accept.

Twelve years after the war, while on a brief visit to London, I was invited by Sir Anthony Eden to his London home just before he became Prime Minister. After enquiring kindly after 'Dear old Uncle Bill Jordan' Mr Eden soon started talking about our days at Tangmere. He remembered many of the boys, and he had not forgotten my proposal that he should become Air Commodore of 486. He wondered why the scheme had foundered.

I had never felt more acutely embarrassed. For the first time in my life I was suddenly elevated on to the battleground of high politics. When your own prime minister has already cut you off at the knees you are at a decided disadvantage, and I left Mr Eden feeling not only humiliated but sadly disillusioned.

4
Mixed 'Operations'

Some people deride superstition. But then most of them have never flown. I am not ashamed to say I always carried a small pink elephant in my pocket; not the one so many people believe they have seen, but a simple little inch-and-a-half-long solid glass elephant, with a broken trunk that had been given to me by a well-wisher before I left New Zealand. An old Danish couple had also given me a gold ring which had travelled round the world several times in old windjammer sailing ships. They considered that if it could survive those days, it could outlive anything. 'Keep it on your finger, my dear boy, and God will return you to your native shores.' To disregard such a message one would have needed a heart of stone.

One morning, flying for Le Havre and already halfway across the 70-odd miles of sea, I suddenly discovered I was without my elephant. It gave me a most uncomfortable feeling and soon afterwards we were in a living nightmare.

As we flew towards the harbour entrance we came upon a fairly large ship. We circled just out to sea, and it showed no sign of resistance. There was nothing to suggest it was a dreaded Spurbrecker, but her captain and crew were well drilled and fully understood my tactics. Suddenly, as I was well down on my run to the target, the whole ship erupted in a blazing display as flak came pouring up. It was too late to call off the squadron, and I lost three pilots within seconds, including my No 2, P/O Norman Preston. I actually felt the shell that plucked Norman from the sky, and collected some of its shrapnel in my own aircraft. As we limped back to Tangmere, with my own Typhoon in trouble, I felt as if someone had hit me in the face with a shovel.

Preston was a similar type to his close friend Fitzgibbon, who had been killed while flying as my No 2 only a few days earlier, and no leader could ask for more faithful followers. Both were strong silent types, and both excellent pilots. When flying as my No 2, or 'wingman' as our American allies called them, they would stick to my tail no matter what stresses I put on my aircraft.

Like most New Zealanders, Norman Preston was a great lover of thoroughbred horses, and only a day earlier had asked me to help him name a young racehorse he shared with his brother back in New Zealand. I thought Focke-Wulf might be appropriate, but after weighing up the pros and cons, we finally settled on 'Typhoon'. It is sad that Norman should be killed in a Typhoon while his horse, which bore the same name as his aircraft, lived to become one of the greatest New Zealand racehorses of its time.

Telepathy, like superstition, is also often ridiculed. Almost two years earlier, I had serving under me an Auckland boy named Bruce Hay. We were on night operations—working out of Manston, near Margate. Bruce was a tremendous all-round sportsman and we both loved rugby. He was the sort of fellow to have around when things got rough—in the sky or on the ground.

I had been flying myself almost to a standstill at about that time, and Wally the station doctor, a good friend to both Bruce and myself, ordered me on a week's leave. I went up to Edinburgh to visit a cousin, but after only three days a strong premonition that something dreadful was about to happen decided me to disregard the doctor's orders and return to my station. The train left Edinburgh at midnight, and after a few drinks with an old friend, Jock Blount, who served in the Argyll and Sutherland Highlanders, and who also knew Bruce, I scambled aboard the train just as it was departing.

I sat in a corner of one of the carriages and soon went to sleep. At precisely 1.30 in the morning, I was suddenly woken by a vivid nightmare. I heard Bruce call out, 'Boss, I'm on fire!' I could see him trying to leave his Hurricane as it plummeted towards the sea. I stumbled out into the passage and was promptly sick. I do not know what the rest of the passengers thought of me, but since they were nearly all soldiers and sailors, I guess they thought that I had become a little 'flak happy'.

Immediately the train pulled into London next morning I phoned Manston and asked Wally if anything had happened to Bruce the night before. There was a long pause, then he answered: 'I thought you would know. He was shot down off Dover at half-past-one this morning.'

*

On 12 July we beat up Bernay airfield, south of Rouen and halfway between Lisieux and Évreux. It was not one of our better efforts, but at least we all got back. Two days later we were on our way to Fécamp in search again of the elusive E-boats, when, some miles northwest of Le Havre we came upon two dinghies carrying eleven American airmen. They had tied the large circular dinghies together, and as we circled low over them I could have sworn they were competing in a game of crap. I radioed for assistance and hung around until an Air Sea Rescue Walrus arrived. It was not big enough to accommodate such a big American crew, so we kept a standing patrol over them until they were picked up by high-speed rescue launches later that day. Most crews we saved dropped us a note of thanks, but not this one. Since they were closer to the enemy coast than to our own, I sincerely hoped they did not resent our intrusion.

The next morning, 15 July, we set out to complete the unfulfilled mission of the previous day, but we came across another bomber crew, this time British and far too close to Le Havre for comfort. I learned afterwards that this bomber crew had been in the water for several days. How the Germans had not sighted them is beyond comprehension.

I left two sections, comprising four aircraft, over the dinghy and hurried back to Tangmere, for if ever there was a challenge this was it. I knew the reaction from HQ 11 Group would be for an international distress call to be sent out immediately, but I spoke to Air Vice-Marshal 'Ding' Saunders and, although he was against it at first, he allowed me the responsibility of attempting a rescue. The Air Sea Rescue boys were soon on their way in a Hudson, under which was slung a special airborne lifeboat, and we made our rendezvous with them off the south coast. We escorted the Hudson to the dinghy, where I instructed the other two sections to return to Tangmere and refuel.

The Hudson dropped its lifeboat which floated down on three huge parachutes. As it hit the sea, two covered areas in the stem and stern inflated automatically. These looked quite comfortable and well capable of transporting the six survivors back to safety. It appeared to have two outboard motors built into wells amidships, for soon after the crew had scrambled aboard I saw one of them starting up the motors. Within minutes they were cruising off on the 60-mile trip home.

Everything was going to plan, and as we circled low over our new charge the moles at Le Havre faded into the distance and the hot sun was making me feel sleepy. Suddenly I was brought up with a jolt when Jim McCaw cried out: 'Sir! There are about a dozen bandits above you.'

I looked up and sure enough the duck-egg-blue bellies of a pack of Huns were circling directly above. They had the drop on us and I had the feeling normally associated with nakedness. But they did not seem keen to take the plunge. The others had returned from Tangmere by this time, so we made eight in all.

I slowly circled away from the lifeboat and when we were well clear of it I instructed the boys to follow me and listen carefully for my command to 'break'. As soon as I straightened out, and we were more or less back in our pairs, the 109s and 190s pounced down on us. At the first sign of tracer I yelled out 'Break!' and swung up to port. I realized immediately that I had forgotten something when a 190 overshot and crossed to starboard right in front of me. I pressed the firing button, and as he flew through my fire I hit his slipstream and was thrown into a spin. Of all my close squeaks this must have been the closest, for in recovering I almost collected the pilot of the FW 190 as he was thrown from his aircraft, a split second before the plane hit the sea. This spin-off was of my own making. While mentally mapping out my tactics I had forgotten to move my coarse cruising pitch into the fine position.

I never saw any of my cannon shells hit this aircraft, although Fitz, in close attendance as usual, was sure they had. Jim McCaw, who was also near to me, said later that my prop missed hitting the water by inches. Pilot Officer Sames shot down an FW 190 and Spud Murphy and Umbers damaged another. Altogether we came out of it quite well. That night, Lord Haw Haw, broadcasting from Berlin, announced that a furious air battle had been fought over the Channel near Le Havre. Well, it had not been all that big in terms of numbers, in fact quite small, but it had certainly been close for me.

Air Sea Rescue launches met the lifeboat 30 miles off the coast and towed it into Newhaven. Wing Commander N. A. N. Bray, commander of the ditched Wellington and a friend of Paddy Crisham, insisted that 486 Squadron be given the lifeboat's centreboard, which we later turned into our official scoreboard. Two or three days later I received a moving letter from Bray, signed by each member of his crew. Written at the navy sick quarters at Swanborough Manor near Lewes, where they were convalescing, it made me feel quite humble. Bray's salvation was all too short, as he was killed a few months later.

*

Every member in some way contributed to the tremendous spirit of comradeship which suffused the squadron. I remember the day when Pilot Officer 'Happy' Appleton arrived. His father was Sir William Appleton, Mayor of Wellington, New Zealand's capital city. Whenever a new boy was posted to fill a vacancy I would spend half an hour with him in my office, so that I could learn something of his experience and service background. 'Happy' was tall, sandy-haired, freckle-faced, with pale blue eyes fringed by almost white eyelashes. It was his hair that intrigued me most. It stood out in all directions like a hedgehog's bristles.

His smile left me in no doubt as to how he had acquired his nickname, but I simply had to tell him to do something about his hair.

'But I've just done it, Sir!'

'Well go and do it again. Try parting it in the middle!'

He took me literally and returned to my office some time later looking like Dagwood, with his hair plastered with Brylcream and sticking out flat on both sides of his head. He looked at me with his pale-blue eyes beneath those white eyelashes as if seeking my approval. I found it impossible to keep a straight face and quickly dismissed him.

That cheerful smile was a great boost to squadron morale, particularly when the days were dark and stormy. Unfortunately, 'Happy' stopped smiling some months later when he was shot down and had his jaw broken in 17 places.

B Flight possessed a sergeant pilot with the uncommon surname of Froggatt. His squadron nickname was obvious, but strangely he had a wide mouth which made the name highly appropriate. Whoever selected him as a fighter pilot must have been looking the other way. I could picture him at the controls of a Stirling or a flying boat, but certainly nothing fast. Short, thick-set, and as grey as a badger, he gave his age as 31, but I am sure he had deducted ten years.

No pilot over the age of 25 was normally permitted to fly in No 11 Group, although there were exceptions, especially among the squadron leaders and wing leaders. I let 'Froggie' fly on defensive patrols, and took him on one shipping strike to qualify him for his Air Crew Europe Star. He arrived back with a cine film of the rear end of Flight-Lieutenant Waddy, and since our cameras were coupled to our cannon mechanism, I'm afraid Froggatt's mind had been well away from the scene of action. However, we could not do without him, and I was glad he belonged to us, because his life would have been short had he been employed on offensive and low-attack missions.

He was the 'head man' of the sergeant pilots, and I think he was also father confessor to some of my younger officers. If he was not engrossed in a game of chess with 'Woe' Wilson, he would be doing something to ensure the comfort of our dispersal. He possessed the driest sense of humour imaginable and was also as cunning as a Maori dog, which I guess in squadron terms means he was a man of superior intelligence.

The remainder of July was taken up in sweeps and Bombphoon attacks on Poix, Abbeville and Caen Carpiquet airfields, although we varied things a bit on 18 July when we escorted two Mustangs as far as Deauville. These two aircraft were flown by two real stalwarts of Fighter Command—Squadron Leader J. A. F. Maclachlan, who had lost an arm over Malta, and Flight-Lieutenant Geoff Page, who had been badly burned about the face and hands. Both were indomitable. They had talked their way back into operations and teamed up to carry out long-range penetrations into French territory.

The idea was to cross the French coast at ground level, and then for them to make their way at nought feet to the training airfields south of Paris. The main problem was crossing, and they asked about the possibility of my lending them some assistance. I had known Mac for some time and had heard a lot about Geoff Page too. For men like them I would have done anything.

I suggested we would accompany them, but instead of crossing in at the same spot and altitude, we would pull up and to port or starboard in order to draw any flak in our direction. On the first trip the plan worked like a charm. The Huns threw everything at us as we beat up some coastal fortifications along the beach west of Deauville. The Mustangs skipped in low without a shot being fired at them. They carried on and had a field day among the Buckmasters south of Paris.

We tried the same operation at a later date, but this time we crossed right on into France ourselves and had a good view of the two Mustangs to port and below us. Neither had any sign of flak around them, but one began shooting out white puffs of smoke from its exhausts—the tell-tale sign of a glycol leak. It carried on for a while and then made a crash-landing near a wood. It was Mac. He was taken prisoner and later was killed while trying to escape. Page carried on, but was hit by flak and forced to make a belly landing when he returned to Tangmere.

*

The flaming days of August were by no means the most productive. Although we made raids of some sort almost daily, only a few stand out in my memory—a hot reception as usual over Poix, and a rough and anxious trip back from Arras when we were stretched out escorting 40 Boston bombers. Acting as withdrawal cover for this operation, we were unfortunate in that the close escort wing of Spitfires did not turn up, so we had to shepherd the bombers out on our own. Enemy fighters niggled at us all the way back to the coast, but there was nothing we could do about them, for if we left the bombers it would have been open slaughter for the 190s and 109s queuing up in our rear. Whilst shepherding a straggler I saw a stream of tracer fly past my my starboard wing, but that was as close as the Huns came to us.

Once the Bostons were over the Channel off Le Touquet I felt much happier because we were now in a position to mix it with the enemy. But when we turned back to meet them they veered off towards France and were soon lost to sight, except for a solitary 109 which continued climbing above Étaples, even though he was being pursued by his own flak.

The Bostons must have been quite pleased with our efforts, for we were asked to fly close escort for them on another raid to Béthune, and to fly rear support for a large raid on St Saëns on 2 September.

We undertook a most unusual operation in the early afternoon of 4 September. I had taken the squadron on a roadstead operation to Fécamp, around the Baie de La Seine, and then on to Cherbourg. Outside Cherbourg we came across a tug towing a target in practice shooting for the German shore batteries. The boys could not leave it alone and as well as giving the tug a fair raking, we left the target in very poor shape.

On 4 September we took 18 Mitchells to Boulogne and got them home safely, even though the flak was murderous. When you can hear flak, then you know it is getting close. Waving to one of the Mitchells' pilots, I had one burst so close it nearly tipped me upside down.

We took some Bombphoons to the marshalling yards at Serquex and, after the bombs were released, straffed the target. Soon afterwards we met tragedy. Pilot Officer Fitzgibbon, my No 2, was killed. We had left the target and were crossing out near Étretat when I spotted an E-boat making high speed towards Fécamp. This was too good to ignore, and I put the squadron in echelon to starboard and peeled down to catch the E-boat in a full-blast cannon attack.

When I pulled up and to starboard to see how Fitzgibbon was faring, he had cleared the target and was rapidly gaining on me. Suddenly his tail came off. I do not know of anyone who survived losing a tail, and Fitz did not have a chance. As he hit the sea I could not believe it. It was a heavy-hearted homecoming, for Fitz had stuck with me through thick and thin, and I felt his future held great promise had he lived. He was quiet, unassuming, and an excellent pilot.

Five days later it was my birthday. As far as the weather was concerned it was not the best sort of day, but I just had to do something. I asked for volunteers to accompany me in a shipping search in the area where we had lost Fitz. Needless to say, the whole squadron volunteered, but I settled on the usual number of eight, half from each flight.

By the time we had crossed-out over the coast the weather had improved and I made straight for Le Havre. As we approached the port I sighted an E-boat moving at full speed towards the moles. It looked a bit close in to be comfortable, so I instructed the squadron to remain out of range while I made a lone attack. As I dived down, I could not believe my eyes, for the boat was swarming with military personnel. I figured it must have come across from Ouistreham on a liberty run. As soon as I opened up there was a mass exodus as humanity in all its shapes and sizes began diving into the sea in all directions. The first burst sent the boat careering round in tight circles, obviously out of control; then it stopped altogether.

Flak came flying out from Le Havre, and as I pulled up and away my heart sank. The rest of the boys had disregarded my instructions and were belting into the vessel with all their might. I had visions of losing the lot, but somehow they survived and we made our way back to Tangmere. Behind us the smoking, sinking wreck of the E-boat was tangible evidence that Pilot Officer Rod Fitzgibbon had been well and truly avenged.

My birthday may well have had its high spots, but that evening I did not celebrate in the mess bar. Instead I lay on my bed and allowed my thoughts to drift back over the years. I remembered the 38 young pilots who had set out so hopefully from our OTU in Lincolnshire. There were few of us left now. I thought of Fitz and of Bruce Hay, Ces Ball and my old cabin mate, Mun Walker. How many of my present squadron would survive the year?

Suddenly from the next room I could hear Squadron Leader Jacko Holmes of 197 Squadron—who normally never stopped laughing—

humming a familiar hymn. It took me back across the oceans, to the little old chapel at Cathedral Grammar School in Christchurch. I suddenly felt the weight of the years, and try as I might, I could not hold back the tears.

Three days after my birthday we were again involved in a slashing attack against a convoy. We had completed what might have been a scenic tour of the Channel Islands, and after passing the island of Sark we crossed over the Cherbourg peninsula to have a look in the Baie de La Seine before heading back home. Soon after arriving in the bay, we came upon an ocean-going tug, a naval escort vessel, and several E-boats and R-boats. We ripped into them and soon two of the lighter-skinned craft were stationary and on fire. Frank Murphy hit the tug, setting off a huge stern explosion. I was hit by flak, but considering the size of this flotilla their reply was rather disappointing.

The next day we took some bombers to Eyas Sud airfield, but that was virtually a taxi ride. The following day, 16 September, we escorted a force of Mitchell bombers to the power station at Rouen. Again I was hit by superficial shrapnel, but my instruments remained steady and I completed the mission without further trouble.

After we crossed out at St Valéry I looked down and saw a small red flare, hardly more than a pinprick on the dark and wide expanse of the sea. Because we had used up a lot of fuel escorting the bombers, I told 'Spike' Umbers to take the squadron home and I peeled off down towards the sea with Sergeant Powell, my No 2. After hunting around for a few minutes we came upon a small one-man rubber dinghy, complete with a wildly waving occupant. It was getting late so we went into minimum cruising revs and pitch and gave a 'Mayday' call. Within about half an hour two Spitfires arrived to take over our vigil and we set off for Tangmere. I had cut things fine, but knew that if we left before the Spitfires arrived we might not find the dinghy again. We made Tangmere at dusk. My No 2 ran out of petrol while taxi-ing to his dispersal bay and my own gauges were reading empty.

The Spitfires could not stay long over the dinghy in the dark and the Fleet Air Arm Albacores went out, hoping to drop a larger dinghy and some emergency supplies. They searched the seas all night but could not find the dinghy; nor could the Spitfires find any trace of it the next morning. I was both annoyed and saddened for, since 486 had found him, I felt the pilot belonged to us. Later that day I scrambled off with Umbers and covered the area of sea from Dieppe to half way across the Baie de La Seine in a series of square searches: but without success. We saw a dead body floating face down on the surface, completely naked except for a short pair of officer's black socks. I immediately thought the poor fellow had despaired of ever being rescued and had tried to swim for it.

However, as I turned away from France, some miles north of Fécamp I caught sight of the dinghy, still complete with its passenger. Promptly and triumphantly I informed Operations, and a Walrus amphibian patrolling north of the area was soon on the scene. It was not long before it had its precious cargo aboard and was on its way to Shoreham and safety. Again we landed back at Tangmere almost out of fuel.

The pilot had been in the sea for several days, and the letter he sent me—a simple 'thank you'—obviously came from the depths of his heart. Saving lives is far more satisfying than taking them.

On 23 September we executed a two-squadron sweep around the Bernay, Beaumont, Tricqueville and Caen airfields, and although we sighted a gaggle of 20 enemy aircraft, they kept well out of our way. Later that day we carried out two more Air Sea Rescue missions, helping to recover the crews of two Bostons.

Two days later I was promoted to Wing Commander and became Wing Leader of the Tangmere Typhoons. Although this was a new post, I had in fact been leading the two squadrons for some time, so it did not really alter my normal routine. But it was nice to know that 'Jacko' Holmes's 197 Squadron came under my command as well as 486.

Soon after my promotion I received a call from Bill Jordan, our High Commissioner. He wanted to take me for afternoon tea with the royal family at Buckingham Palace. If I had not known him so well I would have thought he was joking. Visiting the Palace was not entirely new to me, for I had been there to receive the DFC and Bar 12 months earlier, but that had been purely ceremonial.

I met Mr Jordan at New Zealand House in the Strand and we drove off to the Palace. One glance told me that this was no ordinary tea party. When we were ushered into the presence of their majesties, I could see a number of faces that I recognized from photographs. All the royal family was there, including the Duchess of Kent, the widow of the Duke of Kent. I also sighted South Africa's Premier, Field-Marshal Jan Smuts. Bill Jordan treated them all as if they were members of his own family, placing a fatherly hand on my shoulder as he introduced me. Obviously he was popular with the royal family. They liked him for his simplicity. He was the kind of man who would have lunch at the Palace and that evening eat sausages and chips at the New Zealand Service Club.

The Queen spoke with me at some length, particularly concerning New Zealand, about which she knew far more than I did. Embarrassed, I had to admit I had never been to Auckland, nor seen much of the North Island or Lake Taupo, which was famous for its trout fishing and about which the Queen spoke with great authority.

Talking with the Duchess of Kent, I was better informed. She carried that air of sadness that comes with the loss of a loved one. Her husband had been killed 12 months earlier in an air crash, and I could see that he was still much in her thoughts. She asked me if I had ever met him, and I was glad to be able to tell her how I had first met the Duke early in 1941 at RAF Martlesham Heath, where I was serving as a junior pilot in No 3 Squadron. He was an Honorary Group Captain and spent much of his time visiting RAF stations.

The pilots had been briefed to be careful when they shook hands with the Duke, for during his travels he was obliged to shake hands with many people, and the long-term effect was painful. I had been airborne on a Channel convoy patrol during this briefing and I only joined the end of the line-up a few moments before our royal visitor stepped out of his car.

To give a firm handshake was second nature to me, and when the Duke's soft, well-manicured hand became enveloped in mine I gave it a special squeeze; after all one does not meet a duke every day. He crossed his legs and his knees buckled, and I thought he was about to sit on the ground at my feet. I could see by the expression on the sector commander's face that something was amiss, and as the Duke got into his car he was still shaking his hand as if to restore the circulation. I received a rip-off from the sector commander, the squadron commander and my flight commander—in that order.

However, I had the pleasure of seeing him again at Manston 18 months later. He arrived to lunch with us and was introduced to the officers. Bruce Hay was standing next to me, and after the Duke had shaken hands with him, our guest put out his hand to meet mine, then suddenly pulled it away. Wing Commander Adnams, the station commander, looked at me as if I had suddenly developed leprosy, but the Duke quickly put us at ease. He took me by the wrist and said he had not forgotten our previous encounter, for I had a handshake like a bone crusher.

The Duchess of Kent seemed fascinated to hear my story of earlier, happier days, and expressed the hope that we would meet again. Unfortunately that was not to be.

Field-Marshal Smuts came over my way and we had a long conversation. His knowledge of the air war was extensive, and not confined to the European theatre. Of all the people I have ever met it was he who impressed me most. Along with Winston Churchill, Mackenzie-King and Menzies of Australia, he was the kind of man each Commonwealth country breeds only once in a lifetime.

5

Wing Commander

My first operation as a Wing Commander started with a bang and
nearly ended in disaster. On 3 October we were to pick up a medium
force of Bostons at nought feet about 20 miles southeast of St Lô and
act as withdrawal cover through Normandy and out over the Baie
de la Seine.

We made our rendezvous right on time. As we went to orbit on our
joining-up point, the bombers appeared and we took up our stations
—a squadron on either side of the force, 197 to starboard, 486 to port.
We had no trouble except for the odd straggler.

The type of pilot who dragged the chain, so to speak, was a serious
nuisance. If he was in genuine trouble, such as flying on one engine,
it was forgiveable. But pilots who flew out of formation through
sheer lack of training or indiscipline were a constant headache and
would stretch our squadrons to the limit. I think they felt that with
a few of our own fighters about they were quite safe, but looking after
them was worse than taking care of the main bunch. The enemy
would always concentrate on the stragglers, and if he could split up
the escort he could set about the main formation with much more
freedom of action. Many a time I felt like pouring a short burst close
to the tail of a straggler to remind him of his duty to his own
squadron.

On this occasion all went well until we passed to the west of
Bayeux and made our way towards Arromanches. There flak began
flying thick and fast, and I was doubtful that all of us would survive
the curtain of red hot metal. We all hugged the ground as we passed
over the beach. I felt my aircraft stop a piece of shrapnel, but we all
made it out to sea—how I will never know. It reminded me of those
cowboy films where everyone is firing at everyone but nobody seems

to fall. I was just beginning to congratulate myself as we were about to pass Cape Barfleur on our port side when I received warning that two aircraft were in trouble. One was a Boston, the other one of my 486 Typhoons, piloted by Jimmy Sheddan, a nuggety little farmer from Waimate, South Canterbury, and a good, keen, honest, hard-working member of our team.

The Boston did not worry me—it could land on water as if designed for it, and I had seen several of these twin-engined bombers ditch on earlier operations. But no one had ever heard of a pilot surviving a ditching in a Typhoon. Its huge propeller usually flipped it over on its back the moment it hit the water, and its seven tons of almost solid metal went straight to the bottom. Fortunately, there was neither wind nor a ripple on the sea, and I had my eye on both aircraft, the Boston just ahead of me and Jimmy to starboard.

The bomber touched the surface first. It began to bounce, and after a series of frog-leaps, ended by crashing in a great wall of spray. Sheddan piloted his aircraft far more capably. First the tail-fareing began painting a thin narrow white line on the green sea. The line fanned out into a sizeable white wash; then the main body of the Typhoon touched down and wallowed to a sudden stop—just like a speed boat when the motor is switched off. It was almost un-believable, and I felt like screaming 'Well done Jimmy—you made it!' He quickly inflated his dinghy, and as the aircraft sank, sat alone on the wide expanse of sea.

The Boston crew was not so lucky, but managed to make their dinghy before their aircraft also went to the bottom. I gave a fix on their positions and flew on back to Tangmere to refuel and to arrange a rescue. The ground staff serviced our aircraft and we were soon away, linked up with a Walrus Amphibian of the Air Sea Rescue flight from Shoreham. We were to pick up the Boston crew first and then Flight Sergeant Sheddan, but on our way we found another bomber crew.

Both crews were picked up by separate Air Sea Rescue Walruses. In the first Boston to crash, one of its crew was killed. By the time the two rescues were completed, it was too dark to turn our attention to Sheddan, and we had to leave him at sea until the following morning.

Group, as usual, wanted to send out an international distress call for Sheddan, but I fought them over that. He was one of ours, and I was determined to have him back. It was also good for squadron morale when the pilots knew their wing commander would tilt at authority to ensure their survival, no matter what the odds. I phoned 'Ding' Saunders at some length. At first he was adamant that Sheddan was far too close to the French coast; he considered that for one pilot it was not worth the risk involved. But 'Ding' did not know Sheddan as I did, and after promising I would take full responsibility, I was given the go-ahead.

Firstly I contacted the Royal Navy at Portsmouth and asked for a tide check in the Cherbourg area. After a few minutes they estimated that Sheddan's dinghy should hit the rocks at Cape Barfleur at about midnight, and I was informed by a lieutenant-commander that I would be wasting my time even to consider attempting a rescue. Struggling to remain polite, I told him to look after his own affairs. He hung up.

Later I phoned Portsmouth again for an estimated dinghy position at first light the following morning. I was given a point just off Cape Barfleur and told to fly on a course from Selsey Bill at cruising speed for 17 minutes 22 seconds. I also arranged for Air Sea Rescue to send out a boat from St Catherine's Point on the Isle of Wight, and to have it stationed halfway across the Channel in case of further trouble.

I felt as if the weight of the world was on my shoulders, and did not go to bed that night. Instead, I kept counting the hours to dawn.

As it turned out, Jimmy Sheddan did indeed make contact with the rocks that night—as the Royal Navy forecast—and the Germans were out looking for him with searchlights. But every time the beam swept in his direction, the dinghy was providentially hidden in the trough of a swell. Finally the enemy gave up. When the tide turned Jimmy paddled like hell to get away from the Cherbourg peninsula.

Finally the crucial hour for take-off arrived and with three others we set off low for the Cherbourg peninsula. We flew for 17 minutes at 300 mph, and as the seconds hand on the instrument panel clock approached 22 seconds, a small red rocket went up right in my line of flight. There was Jimmy, tossing about in a choppy sea in his one-man dinghy. The slow old Walrus Amphibian duly arrived, escorted by two sections of 197 Squadron, but by now sea conditions had deteriorated. White caps appeared, and I cursed my luck, for we kept losing sight of the dinghy.

Indomitable Warrant Officer Fletcher was piloting the Walrus, and I asked him, perhaps a little resignedly, how he rated Jimmy's chances. Back came the reply: 'I don't, Red Leader, but since it's one of your boys, I'm going to have a go.'

He managed to set down his aircraft, but it nearly disappeared in a wall of water. They hoisted Sheddan aboard and tried to take off again. I had no experience of flying a Walrus, but I could see immediately that Fletcher's task was impossible. The Walrus wallowed in the heavy sea and lost her starboard float. The waters engulfed her, drowned out her engine and caused part of one wing to fold up.

'Dear God!' I muttered, 'Why must you do this to me?' Instead of only Jimmy in the sea, I now had Fletcher and his navigator as well. I remembered the warning 'Ding' had given me, and had visions of the entire Luftwaffe descending on us, plus all the E-boats from Cherbourg. Our high-speed launches had been listening in to our chatter and, taking the initiative, two raced courageously towards Cape Barfleur. I told Jacko Holmes I wanted a maximum effort from his 197 Squadron to keep the rescue boats covered while 486 would circle over the three principal figures in the drama.

Within little more than an hour the high-speed boats arrived. I held my breath as they collected their cargo and felt a great lump in my throat as they started back towards the Isle of Wight. The only man who was not sick aboard the rescue craft—and this included the crew—was Jimmy Sheddan. He figured he had lost everything the night before.

I thought it wise to end the death throes of the old Walrus. It was floundering in the sea, and reminded me of an old plough horse which after a lifetime of faithful service had suddenly broken its legs. After blazing into it with my four cannons, I shut my eyes for a brief moment, said a short prayer, and set off for Tangmere.

No words of mine could ever praise adequately the efforts of Warrant Officer Fletcher of the Royal Air Force Air Sea Rescue Squadron at Shoreham, not only on this operation, but on many others too. You always had the feeling that if ever you were forced down at sea, no matter where, Fletcher would save you. Had he been serving in the army he would have earned a dozen VCs.

I like to think our Luftwaffe opponents purposely kept out of this rescue operation. Irrespective of some people's experiences, I never saw their pilots behave towards their opposite numbers in the RAF without a certain measure of old world chivalry. We loved the excitement of the chase and the challenge of the skies, but it was still a dangerous arena, and the glory of a golden sunset was very often the end of a bloodstained day.

To give the boys a change, I would occasionally take four or five of my squadron to a London show. We saw most of Terence Rattigan's excellent plays and also Noël Coward's *Blithe Spirit*. The Windmill theatre was always popular and we became well known among the players. It was there I came to know a willowy violet-eyed brunette whose stage name was Margo. She was one of the Windmill chorus, and 'acted' as a nude statue in a number of other scenes. She seemed to me the nearest thing to a Grecian goddess I would ever find—in the West End. We became very friendly, but the last time I saw Margo was from a distance. She was leaving the Strand Palace hotel, arm in arm with a Polish soldier.

I had already converted 486 Squadron to a fighter bomber role, and as soon as I was promoted to Wing Leader I wasted no time in switching 197 Squadron from Typhoon to Bombphoon. There were Spitfire squadrons galore in 11 Group and we also had two squadrons of Spitfire Mark XIIs at Tangmere. They were fitted with the Rolls-Royce Griffon engine, and were the fastest Spitfires of their period.

It must have been a very boring time for all Spitfire squadrons at this stage of the war. Their range was limited, and when they were providing escort or escort cover to the 8th Air Force Fortresses, they could never accompany their charges to any depth. The Luftwaffe were well aware of this and seldom attacked the Fortress formations before the Spitfires had withdrawn. Consequently in these early raids the Fortresses suffered murderous losses once the Spitfires had gone, particularly on two raids against the ball-bearing factory at Schweinfurt, almost 100 miles beyond Frankfurt.

After the first of these raids a Fortress made an emergency landing at Tangmere on only two engines and we raced across to the runway where it had stopped to see how its crew had fared. The aircraft was shot to pieces and several of the crew were either dead or severely wounded. Although the first pilot had had his right arm blown off at the shoulder, I was surprised at the comparative lack of blood around the wound. He was still conscious, even cheerful, and as we put him on a stretcher he said to me 'We sure gave 'em hell, Colonel. God bless America.' He died a short time later while undergoing surgery.

Of the 228 four-engined bombers engaged on that raid, 62 were shot down and 138 badly damaged. Even more serious, 599 skilled American airmen lost their lives.

Compared with the Spitfire, the Typhoon was powerful and fast. With four 20 mm Hispano cannons and superior speed we could almost dictate policy. The addition of bombs made the Typhoons even more lethal, and our trips over enemy territory were seldom fruitless. If the weather was against us in our primary objectives we had plenty of secondary targets. Goods trains were always a favourite. Our four cannons would pierce the engine boilers, helping to put the whole enemy railway system in confusion.

The first time I took up a Typhoon with two 1,000 lb bombs, it rather surprised me. The bombs were mounted one under each wing, and the pilot was unable to see them. And such was the power and lift of the Typhoon, he would not even know they were there. Only a short time before we were escorting twin-engined Blenheims whose maximum bomb load was 1,000 lb, usually 4 × 250 lb. This says a lot for the talents of Sydney Camm, the designer of the Hurricane and Typhoon, and its younger and faster brother the Tempest.

Once both squadrons were well drilled in the art of fighter-bombing, the two Tangmere Spitfire squadrons, led by Wing Leader Ray Harries, wanted to join us on our shows. I gladly accepted, adding that they could accompany us on our fighter-bombing missions as anti-flak escort. They did not ask us again.

I posted Spike Umbers and Harvey Sweetman off for a well-earned rest. Each was by this time the proud recipient of a well-deserved DFC. Ian Waddy, a farmer from Blenheim, Marlborough county, took over A Flight and I promoted Alan Smith, an accountant from Auckland, to take over B Flight.

Waddy was the first of his squadron to get into bother with a Bombphoon. We had been on an early-morning raid to Bernay airfield, and for some reason the 500 lb bomb under his port wing had not left its rack. I informed him of this and told him to stay clear of Tangmere until all the aircraft were down and safely in their dispersal bays. Once this was done, I instructed him to fly out to sea, and pull his aircraft up into a near stall, and fire his cannons in the hope that the vibration from their recoil would shake his bomb loose; but the bomb would not budge. He rolled, looped and stall-turned, but still it would not leave its rack.

Paddy Crisham was waiting for our return and joined us in what was without doubt a highly explosive situation. Ian had used up most of his fuel and the bomb was still attached to the aircraft, so I gave him the choice of either baling out over the sea or bringing in his aircraft. He chose to land and I told him to wheel his aircraft on to the runway as gently as he could and not try a three-pointer.

With Paddy and I peering out from the cover of an aircraft bay, Ian brought in his machine at about 120 mph. As soon as his wheels touched the tarmac in a beautiful 'wheeler', the bomb fell off and started bouncing head over heels along the runway in pace with his aircraft. The first bounce took it up above the level of his cockpit and it completed several skips before coming to rest as Ian hurried on down the runway out of its way. As I mopped the sweat from my brow, I could not help noticing that Paddy had also been sweating for Ian.

Waddy was lucky to be alive. When the bomb hit the runway on its side it had apparently damaged a small propeller which was supposed to complete several revolutions before it could set off the detonator that fired the bomb. With this simple piece of mechanism out of action it was reasonably safe, and both Ian and his aircraft were able to pursue their careers for a few more months.

Burns were the greatest dread of all airmen. The worst misfortune I ever saw happened when a young Spitfire pilot skidded to a halt in a belly landing. He did not suffer so much as a scratch, but when he pulled his harness release pin it broke, and he could not get out of his cockpit. Fire broke out to starboard of the engine nacelle. It spread only slowly, but by the time I arrived the boy was beginning to scream, for the fire was finding its way through the floor of his aircraft and burning his legs.

I tried to undo his harness, but I could not see what was holding it. The fire tender was doing its best, but it just could not reach the main seat of the flames. The boy kept appealing and screaming to me and I had another try, although my right hand was already in bandages from a slight burn received while trying to rescue another Spitfire pilot a week earlier. I grabbed the boy's arm and attempted to pull him clear, harness and all, but that was impossible and I finished up with a handful of burnt skin.

The tender finally brought the fire under control, and as the boy's screams petered out into unconsciousness we were able to cut him free and lift him from the cockpit. The only areas of white skin remaining on his red and blistered body were on his back and where the cockpit and parachute harness had criss-crossed his chest and legs. The offending piece of metal that had trapped him and cost him his life was about half an inch long and as thin as a match.

Accidents of any sort were a constant anxiety to every squadron and wing commander, but they were an even greater worry to our

Group Commander 'Ding' Saunders. He was so concerned at the mounting accident rate in 11 Group that he broadcast a signal to all squadron and wing commanders in his group to post out immediately any pilot unfortunate enough to meet with an accident. I had been extremely lucky with 486 and 197 Squadron Typhoons, but a copy of the Group Commander's signal was displayed on the notice board of each flight dispersal, and I verbally warned the pilots of both squadrons that no exception would be made, no matter who the pilot was, nor how unfortunate the case.

One Sunday in every month Tangmere would be host to one of the many London stage shows, such as *Watch on the Rhine*, *Night Must Fall*, or the Palladium variety show. Our own theatre was made from a converted aircraft hangar fitted with seats from a bombed-out cinema. We always invited local dignitaries, and after the show, which usually took place in the late afternoon, invited the cast and visitors to a party and dance in the officers' mess.

While watching one of these shows, sitting between Paddy Crisham and Foreign Secretary Anthony Eden, I heard a loud crash nearby. I immediately excused myself—Gracie Fields was singing 'Ave Maria' at the time—and hurried out. One glance towards A Flight was enough. Two Typhoons, looking as if they had been playing leap frog, were concertina-ed in a tangled embrace, and of all the offenders it had to be Norman Gall. He had taxied into the rear of another Typhoon and the huge propeller of his aircraft had chewed the tail and most of the fuselage off the aircraft ahead of him. It had stopped only inches short of the pale-faced pilot, Sergeant Powell.

It was my sad duty to tell Norman to go and pack his bags. I went back to the show, but my mind was elsewhere. Not only had the squadron lost one of its most popular and experienced pilots but in saying goodbye to Flying Officer Gall I had also lost a loyal and hardworking friend.

Next day, when I stopped by the engineering section on my way to dispersal, I noticed the tailless Typhoon. It was sitting back on its stump, its propeller facing skywards as if praying to Allah. Below the side of the cockpit a ground staff member had chalked some belated advice: 'Watch my rear. Not hers'. Sergeant Powell, who still looked as if he was pursued by a ghost, had become a chain smoker over-night, and I immediately sent him off on seven days' leave.

I had a fortnight's enforced break from operations when Paddy Crisham went to Ireland on leave. Being next in seniority I had to act as station commander during his absence. This may sound quite a mammoth task for an officer hardly out of his teens, but Paddy had things well organized and I found my new commitments rather entertaining.

With the mounting pressure my wing had been putting on the enemy, the station had many official visitors. Also, I had arranged to have an American Thunderbolt flight attached to 486 Squadron to introduce our allies to the art of dive bombing and low attack operations. So the top brass were constantly visiting Tangmere, and this entailed much entertaining. I found this quite a diversion in itself, particularly with the Americans. Their relatively late entry in the air war put them at a decided disadvantage beside their RAF counterparts, but what they did not know, they quickly learned, and their generosity and willingness to co-operate set examples which some RAF men could well have followed. I liked the Americans.

One day, while I was acting station commander, the Inspector General of the RAF, Air Chief Marshal Ludlow-Hewitt, paid us a visit. His PA phoned to say they would be arriving in an Anson piloted by the Marshal of the Air Staff himself, so I had the red carpet out. I was waiting for his arrival at the watch tower when I saw an aircraft approaching from the distant west, flying just below cloud level. I guessed correctly that it was the Air Chief Marshal, but as soon as I caught sight of the Anson it disappeared into cloud and did not appear again until directly overhead. When he landed I asked what sort of trip he had had from Northolt. Without batting an eyelid he looked straight at me and said: 'Very good, Scott. I flew down in cloud all the way.' His young PA gave me a glance of surprised horror, but I did not want to spoil the old fellow's day.

The post of Inspector General is usually the last job the Air Council gives to a senior officer before his retirement. Like a fading actor, Ludlow-Hewitt went out of his way to impress, and he had me hurrying round as he poked his nose into every facet of station life. He had been to Tangmere many times before, he kept reminding me, but this time his own exuberance nearly cost him his neck.

We had arranged to have some new telephone lines connected to Paddy's offices during his absence. This involved taking up the floorboards, and there was a gap of about two feet to the ceiling of the room below. I warned the Air Chief Marshal of this, but he took no notice—or did not want to hear—and bounded up the stairs ahead of me like a mountain goat. He threw the door open and immediately disappeared into the trough.

Fortunately, the ceiling of the room below was made of stout stuff and he did not fall through, but he promptly castigated me for not having warned him! It is not wise for a young wing commander to argue with an Inspector General of the RAF, so I kept quiet. Then he was proved a really fine old chap, for when we were eventually alone after the inspection, he humbly apologized.

I was staggered to discover how little he knew of the flying side of the RAF. On our way back from the Tangmere operations room, which was some distance from the station, he asked me in the car how a Typhoon squadron joined up after climbing through cloud.

'Of course, Scott, when I was leading my squadron in the Great War, I would always fly my scarf.'

I tried to visualize a Typhoon pilot roaring around the skies at close to 400 mph with a scarf flying from his neck, and wondered which would give first, the scarf or the neck.

We had a legless pilot at Tangmere named Hodgkinson. I had heard much about the legless Douglas Bader, but never thought that the Service could contain two of a kind. The red-haired 'Hoppy' belonged to one of the Spitfire squadrons, and was quite a character. He loved his 'hops' as he called his beer, and it was largely because of this that I had a flare-up with Vivien Leigh.

Our usual monthly stage show was in progress, the cast made up of actors and actresses from a variety of London theatres. Noël Coward received a cool reception from the Tangmere audience when he gave a rather too blue version of his 'Don't let's be beastly to the Germans, don't let's be beastly to the Hun'. As the silence from the audience deepened, his face became redder, and after leaving the stage in a huff he failed to show up at our mess party and returned to London.

Well into the evening, 'Hoppy' asked Vivien Leigh if he could have the pleasure of her company on the dance floor. Knowing Hodgkinson, I guessed he might be a little the worse for a beer or two. I never found out what actually happened, but Miss Leigh stormed off the dance floor and cornered me in the foyer, where she gave me a heated commentary on what she thought of Hoppy, the RAF and our beloved station. I could not get a word in and although I felt like calling her a bloody spitfire, I managed to hold myself together. Then I asked her as politely and calmly as I could, 'Don't you know, Miss

Leigh, that the boy you left standing in the middle of the dance floor lost both his legs in the service of his King and country?' She looked at me in wide-eyed surprise, but did not apologize. Instead, she turned on her heel and like her portrayal of Scarlett O'Hara in *Gone with the Wind* set off in full sail and presumably in the same direction as Noël Coward.

The first trip I made after Paddy returned from his leave was nearly a disaster. I had taken the wing on a sweep around the Beaumont, Tricqueville and Bernay airfields and, while approaching Bernay, I noticed two FW 190s taxiing round the airfield. They had seen us, too, for they stopped to one side of the drome. I peeled off, hoping to see that they stayed there and in flames. When down to about 1,000 ft my motor suddenly snuffed out. I immediately switched to my emergency gravity tanks and turned away towards Paris.

I tested both main tanks and discovered from the gauges that one was full and the other empty. Something was obviously wrong: both tanks should have been at the same level—half full. When a Napier-Sabre is suddenly starved of fuel it often develops a gigantic air lock and takes some time to pick up once the emergency supply is switched in. Several Typhoon pilots had been lost because of this.

As the ground came closer I looked round for a suitable field in which to make a belly landing. Just as I was thinking there were none large enough, my motor came back to life with a spit and a roar. I pulled up my nose and turned for home, but the engine cut out twice more, before finally settling down to an even rhythm.

Once clear of the French coast I had to throttle back to minimum cruising revs and boost, as my gravity tanks were barely sufficient to see me back to Tangmere. I had been so busy looking after myself I had forgotten to detail a section to polish off the two 190s on Bernay, and the boys, worried about my predicament, had stuck close to me all the way home.

What had nearly caused my downfall was a small non-return valve in my starboard fuel tank. An inch or two of faulty brass could well have put me behind barbed wire, or worse still cost me my life. It was my own fault. I should have checked both tanks on approaching the French coast.

On 24 October we attacked six 109s on the airfield at Bernay, but we did not hang around to see the results, for I had stopped a piece of flak somewhere in my tail section. There were no telltale columns of smoke rising from the airfield, so I guess we did not achieve what we had set out to do.

The next day was much better. We raided Maupertus airfield. The flak was so intense that six of 486 Squadron were hit, but our bombs fell in the general target area. On the last day of the month we attacked the airfield of Lissay and scored a near miss on a large hangar; most of our bombs appeared to be spread over the area of the target.

By this stage we had adopted my own style of airfield bombing. It was relatively simple. On approaching the target at 6,000 ft, I would echelon the lead squadron to starboard while the others orbited. Once I was over the centre of the target, I would let it slide under my port wing, count up to seven, roll over and begin my dive.

It was often necessary to screw my aircraft to bring the target into line with my reflector sight; once this was done I would hold it there until down to about 3,000 ft. I would then press the button for bombs away and start my pull-out before climbing rapidly back up to 6,000 ft, which was the most comfortable height and where I could immediately position myself as master of ceremonies. It was at the extreme range of most of the light flak and the heavy calibre always seemed to burst well above this altitude.

I would continue orbiting the target and use my radio to make sure each pilot was directly above the target before he peeled off for his dive. I found the radio procedure most essential, particularly when leading more than two squadrons. If I were leading up to four squadrons the tail-enders always seemed to be in too much of a hurry to get rid of their bombs.

This 'master' bomber technique was responsible for a much neater pattern, and fewer bombs were wasted. I also insisted that each squadron reform after bombing, and did not leave the target area until the complete wing was in its battle formation. If any enemy aircraft scrambled from other airfields we were then well prepared to meet them, and formed a tidy workable opposition.

Low-level bombing was a different matter. It was also much more dangerous. I preferred the steep dive to a low-level approach, and avoided using the latter whenever possible. For low-level attacks, bombs were set at various delays, but even then they could still be fatal to their carrier. You approached your target at nought feet and when almost on it rapidly climbed to at least 300 or 400 ft to give yourself the necessary angle to make your bombs 'stick in'.

This height was the most critical in the face of light flak. If you approached the target at too shallow an angle to keep below the flak, the bombs would not bite in but ricochet and bounce. This could blow you and your aircraft to smithereens. Even bombs with a few seconds' delay could blow up following aircraft still on their own bombing run. So I shied well clear of this type of attack, unless it was against shipping, when the risk was often worth the effort.

We lost a 197 Squadron boy while he was joining up with the wing on the Tangmere circuit, just prior to setting off on a raid against Caen Carpiquet. As usual we were at nought feet to keep below the enemy's radar screens. The boy must have been playing about with the bomb release switches, for both bombs fell from his aircraft and blew him to pieces—along with a man with horse and dray who happened to be below.

The Air Ministry asked me to go to the Midlands to give a lunchtime pep talk to the staff of a factory, Turton and Platts, which manufactured sleeve valves for our Napier Sabre engines. Apparently the factory management was having a difficult time trying to meet its Air Ministry commitments. I thought the cause of the trouble was that the staff, mainly women, just did not realize what an important part they were playing in the overall conduct of the war, so I did my best to convince them of the importance. Later that morning, on the way to a nearby hotel with the managing director for lunch, our car was brought to a halt by a woman leading a beautifully groomed wire-haired terrier. As she crossed the road in front of us I remarked what a fine looking dog it was. I was quite an authority on wire-haired terriers, my mother having owned one for 16 years.

Two weeks after my factory visit I received a scroll through the post. It was signed by hundreds of Turton and Platts workers, and attached was a letter informing me that a four-month-old wire-haired terrier had been dispatched to me by rail. His pedigree was enclosed, and they had given him the registered Kennel Club name of 'Napier Sabre'.

When he arrived, he was all I had expected, a young replica of the dog we had seen in Manchester. He already had a pronounced beard, and his leggings, straight back, perpendicular tail and air of a canine buzz-saw were typical of his breed. Two sniffs—one on either shoe—and our relationship was cemented for life. I could not call him Napier or Sabre, for neither name seemed to suit him. So I named him Kim, and as Kim he became known all along the south coast and in most areas from which Typhoons were flown.

It may seem contradictory, but the life of a wing commander, particularly a group captain, can be very lonely. There are times when you must live with yourself, and by yourself, and Kim brought me that measure of understanding and comradeship which only a dog is able to bring.

Kim took to squadron life and loved flying. When I took him up in a twin-engined Anson he would sit beside me in the co-pilot's seat as if he were fully qualified. Flying low over the Sussex countryside was his idea of heaven. If he saw people and animals in the fields below, he would run barking towards the tail of the aircraft as they swiftly disappeared beneath us. The only flying he did not appreciate was when I put on positive or negative G. If we were flying with a bit of altitude, and I suddenly pushed the control column forward to negative G, it would put him into suspension like a man in space. He could never understand why the floor should fall away from under him.

He developed an almost human understanding. As soon as I put on my Mae West before taking off on a mission, he would put his tail down and slink into the 'spy's (interrogation officer's) office to hide under the desk. There he would stay until we were approaching Tangmere on our return. He seemed to sense just where we were, for often other squadrons would land during our absence and he would not budge an inch. When we were some miles off, and certainly still out of hearing, he would get excited and start whining. As soon as I landed and had parked my aircraft, he would wait until the propeller stopped then put on a performance of sheer *joie de vivre*.

Kim was my constant companion for the next eight months. Then, on his first birthday, he was stolen from my car. With the help of the press and police his abductor was apprehended some 200 miles away, but I never saw Kim again. The thief was a Canadian Air Force mechanic who claimed he had given the dog to a small girl on Broadstairs railway station; however, the police reckoned that Kim was probably sold in London's Petticoat Lane. He was irreplaceable.

Kim was not the only dog at Tangmere. Spike Umbers owned a chocolate-and-white dog called Alfred, or Fred for short. He was a short-haired, long-tailed, ferret-faced mongrel whose white feet seemed to belong elsewhere, and he always seemed to look on me with a marked degree of suspicion. Squadron Leader 'Dizzy' Allen, the station gunnery officer, was the proud possessor of a pure-white portly bull terrier by the name of Crippen. 'Dizzy', a pre-war regular, was one of the few officers who lived off the station; his cottage was near the main gateway to Tangmere, and Crippen seemed to spend more time asleep in front of the officers' mess anteroom fire than he did at home.

Crippen was a most unusual dog. His expression seemed to convey that he was suffering from an incurable hangover, and he treated us all with an air of indifference, as if we were there as temporary guests, which unhappily in many cases proved to be only too true. He loved human company, but never set out to make his presence felt as do many other dogs. I believed he preferred to feel he was just one of the boys and, like his master, was somewhat reserved. If Crippen were laughed at he would bare his teeth and swear vociferously, though I never saw him attack anyone.

Crippen's master was to me a 'true blue' English aristocrat: very polite, beautifully spoken, suave, but not the least pretentious. Although younger, I was senior in rank to him, and I often wondered when he saluted just what he thought of some of us rather raw-boned colonials.

One day 'Dizzy' was posted to Lincolnshire on a short refresher course. For the first couple of days Crippen was quite lost, peering in and out of the mess and even waddling over to the various dispersal huts. Then one night we were celebrating the destruction of two FW 190s over the Isle of Wight by Spud Murphy and Arty Sames. After the bar was closed, we repaired to the anteroom for a cup of cocoa before setting off for our beds.

At that time many Typhoon pilots were severely affected with facial impetigo, caused, we found out later, by a combination of new oxygen masks plus the hot house cockpit conditions of our low-flying operations. The remedy was gentian violet, a bright purple ointment which would stick like clay to a blanket.

Crippen lay asleep in his usual place by the fire, but it was not long before I had him by the collar and lined up for his share of gentian violet. He stood quite still and seemed to enjoy the attention lavished on him by so many of his messmates. First we gave him a great purple ring around his right eye. A backbone and several healthy ribs followed. But the *coup de grâce* was his rear end. After a liberal coating of the grand elixir his ample testicles stood out like a pair of purple light bulbs. By this time none of us could stop laughing. Crippen, fed up with the whole proceedings, wrenched himself free and growling loudly, waddled out of the mess.

Next morning we were at breakfast in the dining hall when Crippen suddenly appeared in the main entrance and with legs well braced surveyed the scene like a defiant Churchill, his right eye peering coldly through its purple frame. For some moments he stood his ground, but as the laughter mounted, he flashed his teeth, turned slowly, and with a mistrustful backward glance retreated, his rear end shining out like a homing beacon. Pandemonium broke loose, as well as a few dishes. One WAAF waitress almost collapsed while carrying a large tray of bacon and eggs, and was only saved from disaster by 'Happy' Appleton.

For several days Crippen was conspicuous by his absence. I later discovered that he was a prisoner of the bathtub and it was not long before the story got back to 'Dizzy' that his wing commander had been the ringleader in this colourful incident. His visits to my office suddenly became less frequent and, when it was necessary to see me, his manner was apt to be over-polite.

As far as I know, both Alfred and Crippen survived the war. Like all of us who shared that Tangmere summer of 1943 they had their failings, but they also helped towards fostering a comradeship which has been the fighting man's reward throughout history. Most of the boys who flew in my wing fell from the skies before the war's end, and I shall forever be grateful for sharing with Kim, Alfred and Crippen the joys and sorrows that were an integral part of the greatest RAF station of all time.

6

A New Enemy

November 1943 began with a bang. On the evening of the 2nd, while
sweeping around the Baie de La Seine just past Trouville, at the
entrance to the Seine Estuary, we came upon the biggest flotilla of
E-boats we had then encountered. It was too good to be true. There
was plenty of light left, and they were far enough to sea to keep us
clear of the shore-based flak. It seemed incredible such a large fleet
of thin-skinned craft should take to the sea in daylight without air
cover.

I told Jacko to keep watch over us with 197 Squadron and led 486
down in a wide circle round the flotilla. Flak came flying up, but we
were still at extreme range and it curved away under us like spent
fountains of red-hot coals. The E-boats were in three line-astern
formations, and once we had them surrounded they seemed to hesi-
tate, as if trapped and wondering what to do next.

The expected lull came in the volume of tracer; I gave the order to
attack and we descended from all directions. I buried my own reflector sight into one of the leading boats which was firing at a
Typhoon to the left of me. My first burst stopped its guns immediately. I quickly gave it another burst. There was an explosion
amidships, and it seemed to lift out of the water and stopped dead
in its wake. I pulled up almost vertically and swung down again on
to a boat to starboard of the flotilla. While I was racing towards it,
several of its crew dived overboard and were soon swamped in white
geysers, explosions and smoke.

I came round for another attack, selected a boat out of control but
still firing its guns, and closed in. I was about to press my gun button
when another Typhoon flashed directly in front of me with cannons
blazing. Typhoons were everywhere and fearing a collision I in-

structed 486 to break off and reform on me to the west of the battle. Jacko and his 197 boys completed their attacks, and as we headed back towards Tangmere, into what was left of a golden sunset, I felt we had at last mastered the seaborne wolves of the Baie de La Seine.

It was at this stage that a new enemy appeared. Our reconnaissance aircraft had photographed several strange sites in the Pas de Calais, and it was suspected they were connected with a new self-launching type of flying bomb. I had a long talk on the scrambler phone to the operations staff at No 11 Group HQ, and it was agreed I should take a look at one of these sites on the evening of 5 November. I took 486 Squadron along, and when we arrived over the site almost directly inland from Le Touquet, I told them to orbit at 5,000 ft while I went down on my own to investigate.

I expected a warm reception, but not a shot was fired, and I had a fine view of a rather puzzling complex. Unfortunately the main building, which resembled a large concrete shed open at one end, was partly hidden among trees, but a short piece of railway track leading to a ramp was clearly visible. By getting down to almost ground level, and virtually squeezing between two clumps of trees, I was able to obtain a much better view of the building as I flashed past. It appeared to be empty. Men began running in all directions, but I did not fire my cannons. First I took another run at the shed with my camera operating. The third time round I pressed my gun button and fired at the concrete shed.

At that moment two huge white Percheron horses, coupled nose to tail to a driverless dray, took off at full gallop from a wood to the left of me. The horses made straight for a low stone wall. They cleared it, but the dray came to a sudden halt and the horses fell in a tangled heap on the other side. They were soon up and galloped down the road in a cloud of dust as if the devil was after them. I hurried back to rejoin 486 and felt more worried about the two horses than I did about the spasmodic bursts of heavy flak that followed us out to the coast.

I believe this was the first attack ever executed against what turned out to be a flying bomb site. The photographic section collected my movie film and I had another long talk on the scrambler to 11 Group HQ. What I had seen was to alter the whole pattern of our fighter bomber operations. Although we continued to bomb enemy airfields and shipping, flying bomb sites were soon to become our primary objectives.

A few days later, when we were making our way over Normandy

after a bombing attack on Bernay airfield, I lost a 486 boy to enemy fighters. Tangmere operations warned me that a formation of 80-plus Huns was above and to the rear of us, but owing to the large amount of broken cloud it was some time before I caught sight of them. Then a patch of blue sky opened up, and there they were, swarming like bees. I eased back on my throttle a little to make sure I had no tail-enders, and told both squadrons to remain calm and on no account to break formation until I gave the order. A dozen of the enemy dived down out of cloud, but some distance behind us. I was not concerned so much about them, but was more worried about what might be happening directly above us. I kept talking to my section leaders, asking them to keep their eyes open. At such times a leader needs eyes in the back of his head.

Glancing behind I saw a Typhoon break away to starboard. I immediately swung the wing round to gather him in, but two 109s shot down from above and were on to him. It was all over in seconds, and although we gained on the two Huns they zoomed up into cloud. Sergeant Seward shot out of his cockpit like a jack-in-the-box and on the end of his chute dropped away in the direction of Bayeaux. I dared not take my formation above cloud and, obeying the urgent pleas of the Tangmere operations controller, withdrew across the Normandy coast and into the Baie de La Seine. No further Huns were sighted, and I could only presume the 80-plus were of the opinion they had been outnumbered.

I felt sorry for Sergeant Seward, and wondered what had induced him to break formation. Losing him had rather spoilt our average of enemy aircraft destroyed, too. Although we had lost many pilots from flak, he was the only one knocked down by fighters during my entire association with 486 Squadron. Nine enemy to one of our own may sound rather like a Battle of Britain score sheet, but as most of the enemy aircraft we destroyed were on hit-and-run missions, it was not all that wonderful. A sneak raider who approached the south coast of England was generally fleeing for his life by the time we caught up with him, and at sea level too. As the Typhoon was faster, it was simply a case of taking him low from the rear, to use an old rugby expression.

I was nearly blown up on my own runway on our return to Tangmere. Jimmy Sheddan was flying as my wing man and was following close behind me as we made our letdown. As my wheels touched the tarmac I heard a short sharp burst of cannon fire behind me and several high-explosive shells burst on the runway around and ahead. Sheddan had forgotten to turn his firing button to the safe position, and as it was situated on the handle of the control column, he had accidentally given it a squeeze. It was a dejected looking Sheddan who came into the dispersal hut after we had parked our aircraft, but having saved him from the sea a few weeks earlier I had not the heart to reprimand him.

Two years later, after he was liberated from a POW camp, Sergeant Seward came down from London to my command at Lasham in Hampshire. He said: 'Sir, I have come to you to apologize. I disobeyed your orders, and got exactly what I deserved.' Something hit me deep down inside, and it was some moments before I could speak. To think he had made a special trip to see me, a journey to get rid of what had obviously weighed heavily on his conscience, even through the privations of prison life. This was the spirit of his generation. Sadly, in 1947 he was killed while flying a Meteor jet in the service of the RAF.

If ever there were an aerial example of David's struggle with Goliath it came on the morning of 10 November when I led the wing on a dive-bombing mission against Hitler's latest secret weapon—the V3.

The V3 was not an orthodox rocket, but a large shell-like projectile fired from a 400 ft multi-barrelled long-range gun at ever increasing velocity by a series of separate explosions piped into the barrel at intervals. This gave the warload a muzzle velocity of some 5,000 ft per second. With 50 of these guns set deep in a massive concrete dome-like structure near the village of Mimeyecques in the Pas de Calais, the Germans hoped to bombard London every few minutes throughout the day and night.

According to reports, Mimeyecques was surrounded by 56 heavy and 76 light anti-aircraft guns, so apparently Hitler held his new secret weapon in very high regard.

Besides this huge ugly concrete monster, 69 flying bomb sites had been discovered by our reconnaissance aircraft, or through our secret agents; all were in the Pas de Calais. Feverish and extensive construction works were also under way near Martinvast on the Cherbourg peninsula. I could see we were in for a busy time.

As we dropped down into the blazing inferno surrounding the target I could see at a glance that our 500 lb bombs would have no effect against such an impenetrable structure. After releasing my cargo I pulled back up, feeling that the whole show was a bloody and dangerous waste of time.

Ten of my aircraft were hit, and two Typhoons from another wing which followed us in were set on fire. One exploded soon after, but the other made it to the coast before curving down towards the sea and disappearing like a flaming torch just off Cap Gris Nez. I did not see a parachute, and can only presume the pilot was trapped in his cockpit.

In the afternoon of the same day we managed a sweep around our old adversaries, Poix and Abbeville, but none of their boys came up to meet us. On the next day, however, we staged a fighter bomber raid on the headquarters of the Todt organization at Audighen and had a fairly hot reception around the village.

Three days of poor weather gave us a welcome break, but we were soon out after shipping again. Two small coasters had been seen off Ouistreham on 16 November, and after hammering away at these we left one listing and the other on fire. I flew back in the evening to take another look, but both vessels had gone.

By this time I was beginning to feel the strain. I realized I was showing many of the signs I always looked for in my pilots. I was smoking too much; I found it necessary to use two hands to stop my cup and saucer from chattering; I would go to bed exhausted, only to lie awake for hours, and when I did find relief in sleep, my dreams were often shattered by nightmares of flaming flak and I would wake up suddenly with my pyjamas soaked in sweat. Even my little dog Kim seemed to sense when sleep evaded me, and he would leave his chair in the next room and lie by my side, as though he felt I required his comfort.

My training days at Wigram, in far off New Zealand, had long since melted into the past, but at that time I began thinking about my classmates more often. When we boarded our ship, the old *Mataroa*, which was to take us to Europe, of us—all members of the same pack drill squad—had joined in a common pact. A small and obnoxious flight lieutenant had been of the opinion that a few drinks in a local pub to celebrate our 'wings' was very much against King's Regulations, and had had us doing strenuous pack drill almost up to the day we left Wigram for our final leave. I could have murdered the little swine. If only I had him with me now! He could lead my wing over Poix or Mimeyecques, and we would see just what he was really made of. We decided aboard ship that if any of us survived we would make it our duty to get square with him.

But out of the ten delinquents, I was the only one still flying. My cabin mate, the ever-clowning Mun Walker, was the first to be killed.

He crashed in a Wellington soon after his arrival, and was wearing my best pullover when he died. He had sold his own to a *Mataroa* crew member in payment for a crown-and-anchor debt, and I had lent him mine to help keep out the English climate. I would have gladly given him my overcoat too had I known what was in store for him.

Dick 'Armchair' Bullen was the oldest of our class—he must have been at least 23. Dick was shot down off Le Touquet by a 109—the first member of 485 Spitfire Squadron to lose his life in action. The big handsome 'Spud' Murphy had come to grief over the airfield of Kerlin Bastard, on the Brest peninsula, and was a POW. Then there was little Alex Mee. He loved flying so much that he wanted to make a career of it. He flew into a balloon barrage near Hull after returning from a night bombing raid and crashed into the Humber river.

The thin-faced effervescent 'Wally' Wallace—who wore false teeth at the age of 20—almost made it: he was shot down by an intruder off Orford Ness, just as he was coming to the end of his thirtieth and final trip. The two inseparables, Gough and Webb, had both been killed in Bomber Command—and on the same night over Boulogne —while Ces Ball, the unflappable, had collided with another Mosquito over Bradwell Bay.

Last to go was the stout-hearted Kelly, the strong-swimming schoolteacher. He went down in the Channel one morning and, after swimming in its icy waters for most of the day, actually made the shore, only to die soon after the coast guards found him.

I was the tenth member of this once-happy clan. I, too, had come so close to death. It often made me wonder why I should be the one left to carry the torch. Sometimes I felt, particularly when surrounded by my pilots, that I was old enough to be their father, yet many of them were older than me. But they looked to me for their salvation, and every word I uttered was the 'Gospel according to the Wingco'. I, too, had my limitations, and it was just as well that my innermost thoughts were camouflaged behind a healthy and youthful complexion.

As winter approached, with shorter days and poorer weather, we normally found our activities reduced, but this year the ever-mounting threat of Hitler's secret weapons meant that there would be little respite, if any.

Some weeks earlier we had begun to design a 486 Squadron crest. Thanks mainly to Pilot Officer Arty Sames, we had it completed and sent off to the College of Arms for approval. Choosing a motto for this crest was easy. The squadron had started off on Hawker Hurricanes, was now flying Typhoons, and was undoubtedly designated for the new Tempest. We therefore adopted—most appropriately, I thought—the motto *Hiwa Haw Maka*, which is Maori for 'Beware of the Wild Winds'.

The centrepiece was a different matter. Some of the squadron thought a kiwi would be most appropriate, but although New Zealand's national emblem, I strongly opposed this. Not only is it flightless, it is almost sightless, and its beady black eyes and long tapering bill reminded me of a tax collector. Our American allies called it the 'fat-arsed duck'. We settled on the high-flying mountain dweller, the sharp-billed, colourful parrot-like kea, and we had no trouble in getting this approved by the College of Arms. I received word that our crest would be officially presented to the squadron by our group commander, Air Vice-Marshal 'Ding' Saunders, at the end of November.

We raided Bernay airfield again on 19 November. There were few aircraft on the ground, and although our bombs kicked up great clouds of dust in the dispersal areas it was not a successful bombing mission. However, it was good training for some of the new boys.

Our next three efforts were all against the headquarters of the Todt organization at Audighen, the administrative centre controlling some 50,000 conscripted workers engaged on the construction of the V1 and V3 sites in the Pas de Calais. During our first raid, on 20 November, seven aircraft were hit by flak; one crashed into the sea halfway between Boulogne and Newhaven without giving any warning that it was in trouble. The aircraft was in formation one minute, and the next dived straight into the sea. For the other two raids on Audighen there was a considerable strengthening in the flak defences, and our bombing was consequently of a much lower standard.

On 26 November Group HQ asked me to take the wing to bomb Martinvast, some distance to the south of Cherbourg. I was warned that it was heavily defended, and was a similar type of site to the one we had attacked some days earlier at Mimeyecques. If this were indeed the case, I was convinced that it would take the might of Bomber Command and its 12,000 lb bombs to even make a dent in it. By way of a change, I led my wing in from the south against this new target, which meant flying between the Channel Islands and the Cherbourg peninsula, and crossing inland in the vicinity of Carteret.

There was no need to search for the target. A great wall of intense and heavy flak began to climb skywards long before we were in striking distance—the enemy had obviously correctly predicted our height, speed and direction. Weaving under such conditions is quite useless, so I approached the target by varying 20 degrees to port for 20 seconds and then 40 degrees to starboard, at the same time varying height. But there was still the unavoidable run over the top.

Just as we were about to position ourselves, I flicked on my transmitter and was saying 'Now boys, you have seen plenty of this stuff before', when a shell exploded under my port wing and almost tipped me upside down. My message ended abruptly in a four-letter word, and knowing the effect this sudden outburst would have on some of my less experienced followers, I tried to talk calmly to them as I began to peel off down to the target. But I felt my heart pounding in my throat and my whole body was beginning to shake. As I plunged down through the blazing sky, I actually closed my eyes for a moment as the target came up towards me—something I had never done before.

We somehow managed to scramble through this curtain of fire, but many of our aircraft were pock-marked by shrapnel. As we flew on to the east side of the peninsula and into the bay, I could see Flying Officer McCaw weaving to the starboard of me, and I managed to blurt out: 'OK Mack, you can relax now.' I received no acknowledgment, so I guess he was much like the rest of us and too occupied with his immediate future to worry about his past.

'Ding' Saunders arrived at the end of the month bearing 486 Squadron's new crest. While presenting it he had many complimentary things to say about our squadron. Much had happened throughout the long summer of 1943 and as he reeled off our achievements I suddenly felt choked: I was so proud to have been part of it.

That evening after dinner he took me over to a large leather sofa in the corner of the anteroom and told me to sit down. He did not beat about the bush: 'Scottie, you finish operational flying as from today. I want you to take over as station commander at Hawkinge.'

I was thunderstruck. Tangmere had become almost part of me; it was my home. But he did not give me any opportunity to argue.

'I note from squadron and wing records that out of 157 offensive missions, you have led every one except three. That's more than enough for any man. You will enjoy your new command at Hawkinge. Good luck.' With that he shook my hand and accompanied by Paddy Crisham left for Uxbridge and the No 11 Group HQ.

That night I had trouble sleeping. I tried to read, but my mind kept wandering. There seemed so many things I had to do. I must post Froggatt to safer surroundings. McCaw and Waddy had had enough; Bluey Dall and Woe Wilson, too. It was going to be hard saying goodbye to Paddy—and how do you thank your ground staff? Your fitter and rigger? Your very life had depended upon them. I put out the light, buried my head in the pillow, and tried counting sheep.

As it turned out, my presence was required at Hawkinge almost immediately, so there was little time for lingering farewells. I visited all the ground staff and thanked them for the splendid support and service they had given me during my time at Tangmere. They had toiled throughout the long summer days—and often right through the night. No commander could have asked for more.

Saying goodbye to the pilots was much easier than I thought it would be, as I had agreed to attend a farewell party at a later date. That let me off the hook, and I was most thankful. In sharing the dangerous skies you developed a comradeship that only death could conquer, and any goodbye could be the last.

Two days after receiving notice of my new appointment I said goodbye to Paddy, and began my journey to Hawkinge. Some weeks earlier I had bought myself a little Austin car and its 7 hp engine was a far cry from my Typhoon. It had spent the war years in a Chichester garage, and with only 4,000 miles on the clock I had bought it for the princely sum of £40. With my suitcase and bits and pieces on the back seat, and Kim alongside me in the front, it was just made to measure. As we approached the barrier at the gates to Tangmere, I saw Crippen waddling along towards the mess. Kim barked a rousing Good morning at him, but he did not even look our way. The barrier rose before us, a smart corporal sprang to attention, saluted, and said, 'Goodbye Sir, and God Bless You.'

We were soon humming along the road that led to Brighton. After passing through Arundel, Worthing and Shoreham we stopped to stretch our legs. As I was gazing out across the Channel I heard a familiar sound. Looking behind I saw two squadrons of Typhoons approaching rapidly over the tree tops. With a thunderous roar they flashed overhead and soon disappeared over the flat green waters in the direction of France. I stumbled back into my car, suddenly feeling very much alone.

Desmond Scott and 'Spud' Murphy, Tangmere, September 1943.

HRH the Duke of Kent (soon to meet a tragic end) talks to New Zealand Pilots at Tangmere. (IWM)

Bombing up: the Ground Crew at work. (IWM)

Desmond Scott's Typhoon being refuelled, Tangmere 1943. (IWM)

An Air Sea Rescue Walrus.

A member of the Ground Staff at Tangmere shows how a pilot (who survived) ended up after crashing his Typhoon.

The 486 New Zealand Squadron Crest. The motto Hiwa Hau Maka means *Beware The Wild Winds*. The skull cap belonged to Wing Commander N. A. N. Bray whose rescue from the sea is described in the text. The scoreboard speaks for itself.

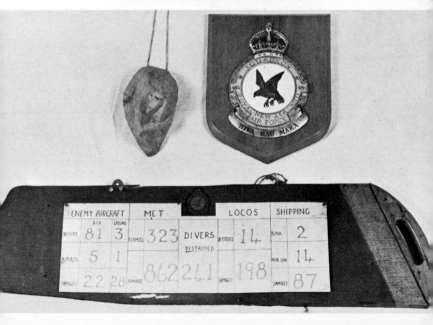

Rocket Firing
Typhoons. (I

A Hawker Typhoon F Mark 1 B with a 2180 hp. Napier
Sabre IIa engine. Normandy 1944. (IWM)

Typhoons lined up on a forward air strip in Normandy. (IWM)

Special warming-up treatment for an RAF Typhoon. Collapsible tubes are used to carry hot air from the pre-heating van. Winter 1944. (IWM)

A Typhoon takes off watched by troops resting on the perimeter of a hastily constructed airstrip. (IWM)

Another view of a Typhoon on a forward airstrip in Normandy. The explosion in the background is caused by a bomb disposal unit 'de-lousing' the outfield. (IWM)

Desmond Scott and Wing Commander W. Dring meet General Eisenhower on an airfield in Holland. Dring was killed a few days later in the Ardennes offensive.

A Typhoon's-eye view of the devastation caused by bombardment and strafing. Note the advancing Allied tanks with their white identification signs. This photograph is of Julich and was taken in February 1945. (IWM)

These two pictures show a Rocket Firing Typhoon attack. A very careful study of both photographs will reveal to the discerning eye tiny shapes of the aircraft themselves. The point of release of the two rockets is indicated by the two white puffs. (IWM)

7

Hawkinge

Motoring along the south coast towards my new command at Hawkinge was an interesting departure from my usual and much swifter means of transport. I knew Brighton, Eastbourne, Bexhill and Hastings well from the air, but had never had the opportunity to explore these coastal towns from the ground. Althought they had all suffered from enemy fighter bomber attacks, the inhabitants were friendly and in no way depressed, Indeed, the great faith they had in our Typhoons was almost embarrassing.

Some weeks before leaving Tangmere I had been awarded the DSO to add to my DFC and Bar, and with this further decoration went a certain amount of publicity. I imagined it was because of this that the people gave me such a warm welcome wherever I went. Walking into a pub in Bexhill and ordering a beer, I was greeted by the landlord with: 'Certainly, Wing Commander Scott.' I looked at him hard and was certain I had never set eyes on him before. I asked him how he came to know my name. He promptly deflated my ego by saying he had recognized me through my dog.

As I approached Hythe, only a few miles southwest of Hawkinge, I was reminded of an incident nearly two years earlier that almost landed me in a POW camp. I had been working out of Manston airfield near Margate, and on top of my normal duties had been selected to do a number of calibration tests on a new type of radar under development. It was referred to as 'Type 16', and from all accounts it could even plot the traffic on the French roads.

All I had to do was act as a target during these trials by flying 100 miles into France at night at a predetermined altitude that had to be strictly adhered to. It was permissible to wander a few degrees either way off track, but the height band was on no account to be broken.

On the night of 29 May 1942 I was happily playing billiards and drinking the odd tankard of beer with other members of the Manston mess. All the lower-altitude trips had been completed over a period of some weeks and I had almost forgotten that the highest trip of all was still to be flown. Then I was called to the phone. It was 11 Group HQ. I was to get myself airborne as soon as possible, position myself at 25,000 ft over Hythe, keep radio silence and set course for France at exactly 15 minutes to midnight.

The weather was lousy and I was puzzled too by the urgency of the instructions. But the almost pleading voice from the 11 Group operations room at Uxbridge left me in no doubt as to the importance of the mission. I phoned our dispersal hut and instructed Sergeant McArthur to warm up my long-range Hurricane, as I would be taking to the air within the next 20 minutes. His response was not encouraging:

'Cor blimey, Sir. Are you kidding? I'll be bloody lucky to find it. It's like pea soup out here!'

Bruce Hay drove me to our dispersal hut. As I climbed out of the car I put my left shoe into a puddle of water. If I had not had a few beers beforehand I might have realized how dangerous it could be to take off high into the night sky wearing a partly wet sock. But I ignored this annoying accident and wrapped myself up in an Irwin suit and donned my Mae West. Climbing into thick cloud above Manston I was soon working hard at my instruments.

Soon, after breaking through a great towering mass of cloud above Folkestone, and as the large hand on my instrument panel clock touched the quarter hour before midnight, I had reached the necessary altitude and was set on a south-easterly course leading me towards France. Above was a bright moon, and below and ahead, as far as the eye could see, stretched an endless unbroken ocean of fluffy white peaks and valleys. Above the turbulent cloud the atmosphere was completely calm and I had no trouble keeping my altimeter stationary at 25,000 ft. The voice of the Rolls-Royce Merlin engine seemed to grow softer as I flew towards my turning point, which should have been within a few miles of Cambrai.

Turning on to my reciprocal course to come home I started to be aware of the cold, particularly in my left foot. I was also overcome by a feeling of enervation, combined with the urge to sing. Deep inside I knew something peculiar was happening, but I just could not put things together. I shook my head and saw that I had already dropped 3,000 ft below my allotted height band. But it was the oxygen gauge that suddenly hammered away at my senses: the needle read empty! Even in my fuzzy state this realization acted like a slap in the face—if I did not get myself down to a lower altitude my fate was sealed.

Had the sky below been clear it would have been simple, but letting down into solid cloud at 20,000 ft in a single-seater aircraft was dropping down into the unknown. As I sank into this great white blanket of cotton wool the moon was suddenly turned off and if ever I was alone with the elements it was during that next half hour. The deeper I went the darker it became.

At about 15,000 ft I flew through a violent hailstorm accompanied by severe buffeting. The hail thrashed against my aircraft, even drowning the sound of the motor. I might well have been walking a tightrope on a dark and windy night, and I had to work desperately hard on my instruments to keep the plane stable until, down to about 5,000 ft, the going was not quite so boisterous.

At 600 ft I broke through in heavy rain. Below me was a canopy of four stationary searchlights. As I turned towards them, they were immediately switched off. By this time I was certain I had recrossed the English Channel and was somewhere in the vicinity of Canterbury. So I flew north for several minutes, hoping to meet the Thames estuary, and began calling Hornchurch control for a fix. But I could not even receive a background, even though all four channels were lit, which meant that my radio was in full working order.

Another cone of searchlights appeared to the northeast, and I turned towards it in the hope that it was Manston. It was obviously not my home base but at least it was an airfield—I could see the runway lights. I circled it several times, thinking that my only—humiliating—course was to drop in and ask where I was. I lowered my wheels and flaps and began my approach.

Then at about 200 ft I suddenly realized I was flying down a visual lorenz. This was a German airfield lighting system and I concluded that I was making a let-down on to one of our dummy airfields—all lights but no place to land—that had been set out by the British to fox the German night bomber force. I had heard of them, but had yet to see one.

I lifted my wheels and flaps, opened up the motor, and climbed into cloud. At 2,000 ft I tried contacting Hornchurch again. There was an immediate response; I could hear a voice, although it was far away in the background. When I climbed higher it came through much clearer, and I was able to hear my own call sign: 'Lochinvar are you receiving me. Vector three two zero. Vector three two zero.' I answered, but they obviously could not hear me, for I kept receiving the same message over and over again.

I let-down below cloud again, and set my compass on 320 degrees, although that seemed rather strange: it would take me in a north-westerly direction—according to my reckoning towards the London balloon barrage. After flying for almost 15 minutes on 320 degrees my radio reception became much clearer, and I was able to acknow-ledge Hornchurch without difficulty.

Several searchlights began probing around, but I soon left these behind as I crossed out over the coast, into what I believed was the Thames estuary. Indignantly I informed Hornchurch that they were sending me out to sea. The controller's agitated reply made the heat surge to my face—but my left foot still felt like a block of wood.

'That's right Lochinvar, I hope we are. Continue on vector three two zero. Continue on three two zero. Buster Lochinvar. Buster!'

'Buster' meant hurry. It was then that I realized I had just crossed out of enemy territory. The airfield I almost landed on must have been in the region of St Omer. No wonder the Huns did not fire at me. I was obviously far more valuable to them alive than dead.

By the time I arrived over Manston my flight plan was about an hour overdue and I had little time to ponder on why I had almost become a POW. As my left foot began to thaw out, the pain became excruciating and I was carted off to sick quarters to be treated for suspected frostbite.

A few days later I was invited to 11 Group HQ to meet some of the backroom boys. They said they had lost track of me at one stage and, in doing so, discovered a hidden fault in their equipment that would not otherwise have surfaced. This discovery proved of great benefit to the radar scientists working on this new system. It sounded rather a tall story, but according to them my trip over France was highly successful, and I may well have saved Britain many hundreds of thousands of pounds.

The afternoon shadows were beginning to lengthen as I passed through Folkestone and started driving behind the town towards Hawkinge. Away across the channel I could see the enemy coast in the region of Cap Gris Nez. Smouldering under a yellow haze it was covered by the rays of the late autumn sun, and I could not help wondering if the E-boat commanders in Boulogne were already preparing for another night's foray into our coastal waters.

I had landed at Hawkinge many times before, and also at Lympne, another airfield some ten miles southwest of Hawkinge, a satellite station also under my new command. Hawkinge airfield lay in a slight hollow on the high ground above the cliffs some three or four miles northwest of Folkestone. A plain grass airfield, it had suffered a heavy hammering from the Luftwaffe during the Battle of Britain, and some of its outlying components had also taken a battering from the big enemy guns from across the Channel. This part of the south coast was commonly referred to as 'Hell Fire Corner', so I had forsaken my Typhoons, but at least I was still in the forefront of the battle, even if it meant flying a desk for the next few months.

I hardly had time to settle in, or even visit two new Typhoon squadrons, No 609 and No 1 based at Lympne, when I ran into my first major problem. A call from a Lincolnshire Bomber Command station informed me that they were railing down to Folkestone the remains of a young pilot officer who had been killed with his crew in a flying accident. I was asked to provide the funeral party and make arrangements to collect the coffin and take it from Folkestone railway station to Hawkinge, where he was to be buried in the local cemetery.

Had the Bomber Command consigners been proficient everything would have been straightforward, but I had a shattering phone call from Folkestone railway station. The officer in charge of the funeral party informed me that the Bomber Command station had sent the wrong body. Since the dead boy's young widow and his parents were also at the railway station, this put me and my staff in a most embarrassing predicament.

I could not leave the body at the railway station, nor could I in any way neglect or cause further anguish to the bereaved. So I instructed my officer to bring the coffin to our own morgue and told him I would send my adjutant in my car to collect the boy's widow and parents. Then I contacted the Bomber station where the boy had been killed. His station commander was already aware of the mistake, as they had just received a similar call from a station in Scotland to say that they had received a wrong body. There was no excuse for such a blunder and I insisted that both bodies be delivered to their rightful destinations the next day, and by one of his own Bomber Command aircraft.

A dejected and bewildered trio came into my office. The young widow, heavily pregnant, burst into tears and began berating me for the mix-up that had added so much pain to a heart already torn to shreds. As soon as she appeared a little more composed I invited my visitors to sit down. The boy's elderly parents sat holding hands and looked at me like two sad-eyed spaniels. The assistant adjutant, a WAAF officer, brought in a tray of tea and biscuits. The soul-searing silence which accompanied this diversion was almost too much for me. Trying to hide my emotions, I left my chair and stared out of the window across the broad expanse of grass airfield. I noticed it was beginning to rain.

Then suddenly I was set on from behind by the young widow, her clenched fists beating a frenzied tattoo across my back and shoulders. Had she been a man I would have known how to handle the situation, but dealing with a young woman, and a pregnant one at that, was something quite new to me. I just stood frozen while she was led away by the assistant adjutant who had luckily returned to my office to see if more tea was required. The mother and father were very upset by this time and tearfully apologized for their daughter-in-law's sudden outburst. Then I almost lost control of myself when the two old souls humbly thanked me, at some length, for the 'wonderful' cup of afternoon tea.

I arranged to have all three driven back to Folkestone and as soon as they left I put up the 'Engaged' sign on my door, locked it, and was thankful to be left alone in silence.

Hawkinge was an interesting station to command, mainly because of its close proximity to the enemy coast. I knew some of the pilots. Flight-Lieutenant Griffiths had been posted from Tangmere to join 501 Spitfire Squadron, which was commanded by another New Zealander, Squadron Leader Garry Barnett, a Wellington accountant. 501 Squadron specialized in 'Jim Crow' patrols—reconnaissance flights over the channel in search of shipping targets for our fighter and torpedo bombers.

Besides an Air Sea Rescue flight of Walrus aircraft, I also had a Dutch Spitfire squadron, No 322, commanded by Major K. C. Kuhlmann, DFC. The officers' mess was not large enough to accommodate all the aircrew, and the Dutch squadron had their own dispersal mess in a large country house some miles from the airfield.

However, after Tangmere, the officers' mess reminded me of an old men's home. It seemed overloaded with elderly administrative officers, some of whom seemed to lack the enthusiasm and sense of purpose which had been so noticeable at both Tangmere and Manston. Many of the staff officers had been at Hawkinge for too long. Some gave me the impression that in their view combat squadrons could come and go, but their own tenure was safe for the duration.

As far as I was concerned, flying personnel came first, and I started sweeping in the administrative quarter with a very stiff broom. Several officers were posted out of the station, and to bring us more in line with our overall operation commitments, I decided that a weekly staff conference be held which senior administration officers were ordered to attend.

This was not a popular move among some of the more senior staff and at our first conference I could sense open hostility when I suggested a number of departures from the normal daily routine orders. This was understandable; most of them were pre-war regulars and had many years of service behind them. Attending meetings chaired by a comparative newcomer—and a very youthful colonial at that—would have tested the professional dignity of most regulars.

Despite the initial difficulties, with the cobwebs swept away and a lively infusion of new blood, we settled down into a more co-ordinated assembly, and I believe that the operational side of the station was much happier for the changes. However, a station commander's life could be very lonely; like a stranger in a big city, I was exposed to its bright lights but still had to weather alone the chill winds that accompanied every change.

Apart from the loneliness, I enjoyed my first few weeks. Sitting behind a large desk was a change from my normal place in the cockpit, but after a while it reminded me too much of my days at Bentley Priory. Like most grounded operational pilots I soon began to yearn for the comradeship of my fellow flyers and the unfettered world of the open skies. Still, there was always something happening on the airfield, and I baled out of my office chair on the slightest pretext. Being so close to the enemy, Hawkinge was a natural haven for many a lame duck, both fighter and bomber. Aircraft short of fuel or badly knocked about by flak or fighters would suddenly descend on us, often with tragic results.

One day I was driving on to the airfield perimeter track with an old school friend down from his Norfolk bomber station for the weekend, when a lone Spitfire with a dead prop made a wheels-up dive for the safety of our smooth grass acres. The pilot almost made it, but could not quite reach the boundary and crashed heavily into a hedge and low bank just a few feet short of the airfield. His Spitfire burst into flames.

The aircraft had hit hard, but the wings were still intact, and I could see from the many jagged flak holes that he had had a rough time. The cockpit was well ablaze and it was some moments before the fire crew could temporarily douse the flames surrounding the pilot. He was unconscious but still alive, although I could see he was badly injured about the face, obviously having smashed against the reflector sight. I managed to undo his safety straps and parachute harness, but the heat drove me back. Then a well-aimed blast of foam again flattened the flames and allowed me to get my hands under his armpits. I found I could lift him up a little way, but something seemed to be holding him back. I called to my friend to help, but he had retreated to my car and was leaning against it being sick.

Things were getting really hot. The crash tender crew were doing their best with the hoses, and although I yelled at them to get in closer, they seemed to be treating the burning aircraft as if it were loaded with bombs. I made a last desperate bid to lift him clear. Something suddenly gave way and the next moment I fell flat on my back on the port wing, taking the helpless body of the unfortunate pilot with me.

With ammunition exploding on the other side of the aircraft, I struggled to my feet. Then I was hit by a jet of foam and almost blinded. It was the best thing that could have happened. As I had bent down to catch hold of the pilot's legs to pull him clear, there was a loud explosion and I felt a searing blast of hot air which singed my lips and eyebrows and briefly set fire to my left trouser leg.

Once clear of the flames, I could see at a glance that our efforts had been in vain. Apart from his burns and severe head wounds, the pilot's lower body and legs felt like rubber, as if they had been broken in a hundred places. He was still breathing, but died before we could lift him into the ambulance.

Feeling hot, wet, sore and dejected, we drove back in silence to the officers' mess to shower and change. My old school friend sat quietly weeping. Remembering his bravery on the rugby field six years previously, I felt disappointed, and could not understand why he had let me down when I needed him most. But I knew that flaming crashes were common on every air force station, and he might well have lost a close friend under similar circumstances.

We both treated the incident as if it had never happened, and the next day, when he boarded the train at Folkestone to return to Norfolk, he was back to his old cheerful self. Four days later his own bomber was shot down. He cleared the aircraft but his parachute failed to open and he met his end near the small village of Loos in northern France.

Some days I would become brassed-off with office commitments, and then I would borrow a Spitfire from either 322 or 501 Squadron and take to the skies above Kent. For the sheer joy of flying, no aircraft could compare with the Spitfire. Whereas the Hawker Typhoon was a classic example of brute strength and ruggedness, the Supermarine company had produced in the Spitfire an aircraft akin to a man-made swallow. It flew as if it were truly born to the heavens. Snug in its narrow cockpit you felt part of it, and while rolling, looping and stall-turning, its smooth Rolls-Royce Merlin engine would accept every challenge without a note of complaint. But I was still very much a Typhoon pilot and I would drop into my satellite station at Lympne and spend an hour or two with the Typhoon boys whenever I could.

When 'Ding' Saunders had taken me off operations at Tangmere I had promised him I would not fly operationally again until my term as station commander was completed. That sounded fair enough at the time, for I was beginning to feel at the end of my operational tether. But after a few weeks' rest I was beginning to wonder whether or not his decision was altogether wise. Hearing a squadron of Typhoons spitting, barking and roaring at each other while queueing up for take off would set my blood afire, and I was often sorely tempted to join their sweeps across the channel.

Many former squadron and wing leaders would probably have disagreed with me, but I became firmly convinced that every front-line station commander should fly operationally with his squadrons, even if only once a fortnight. It would be good for station morale and keep the commander well up with the ever-changing pattern of the aerial offensive. A wing leader might not feel comfortable with his station commander breathing down the back of his neck. However, the fact that the commander was prepared to accompany his squadrons over the Continent would remind his subordinates that it was only through their combined efforts, and no matter at what level, that the war against Germany could be won.

The stations in Fighter Command were still having more than their share of aircraft accidents, and Hawkinge was no exception. The Dutch squadron (322) had had two taxiing accidents in one week, and Saunders instructed me to warn its pilots that if a further accident occurred, the whole squadron would be taken off operations and removed from Hawkinge to undergo a period of corrective training. This was tantamount to shifting them from the top form into the dunces' class, and feeling that they had the potential to become a first-class squadron, I informed them that it would be a blow to me—as well as to their morale—if they were lost to my station.

About two weeks later the inevitable happened. A 322 Squadron pilot carelessly taxied his aircraft into the back of a three-ton truck. 'Ding' Saunders wasted no time and a signal arrived from 11 Group HQ instructing me to inform the Dutch squadron to prepare to move out. Then within hours I received another signal: Prince Bernhard of the Netherlands would be flying in the next morning. As usual, the Dutch royal visitor piloted his own aircraft and arrived at Hawkinge just before our midday mess.

Coming as I did from the other side of the world, I was to naïve to appreciate the political embarrassment that could be caused if the Dutch squadron were suddenly posted out of No 11 Group—Britain's premier fighter group. As far as I was concerned all squadrons were the same, whether Rhodesian, British, Canadian, Australian, New Zealand—or Dutch. We were all members of the Allied Air Force, all striving for the one purpose, all subject to the jurisdiction of the same Air Ministry.

However, I was not unaware of Prince Bernhard's annoyance at the news of 322 Squadron's posting, although it was not until we were in the bar for our pre-lunch cocktails that he mentioned the subject—and in tones loud enough for all his squadron to hear. I was never much of a diplomat, and my answer was a little too short and to the point. Fortunately 'Ding' Saunders had sent his senior air staff officer, Air Commodore 'Daddie' Bouchier, to Hawkinge for the day, no doubt sensing that I might require his diplomacy for just such an occasion. 'Daddie' stepped in to heal the breach, but this did not prevent the luncheon that followed from being a dull affair, the conversation either stilted or non-existent.

After coffee the Dutch boys formed up in a hollow square near the station flagstaff, for an address from their commander-in-chief. After the address he was about to present decorations when the air was shattered by the wail of the emergency siren. Hurriedly excusing myself, I leapt into my car and drove off fast in the direction of the airfield perimeter taxiway. A visiting Spitfire had crashed on its belly, skidded through the boundary fence into a small gully and broken its back. A large column of black smoke conveyed its own sinister message. The Spitfire could not have finished in a more awkward position, and we could not rescue the pilot from his blazing prison. Prince Bernhard arrived and I became more than a little concerned for his safety, since it was impossible to tell whether or not the aircraft had been carrying bombs.

While helping in this rescue attempt I was again almost saturated by the fire tender, and it was a wet and bedraggled host who saw the Prince off to Northolt where he kept his aircraft.

322 Squadron left Hawkinge for Ayr a few days later, to become one of the first squadrons in the Allied Air Force to be equipped with the much-sought-after Spitfire Mark XIVs. It was to acquit itself well in the lead-up to and during the invasion of the Continent.

Twelve months were to pass before I saw Prince Bernhard again. After supporting the Walcheren landings at the entrance to the Scheldt estuary, I shifted my 123 Wing and its four squadrons of rocket-firing Typhoons from Ursel in Belgium to Gilze Rijen in Holland. Prince Bernhard was busy on his home territory and we would often wave to one another while carrying out our respective duties. His shining example in flying himself on his royal commitments was a tremendous inspiration to all members of the Netherland's forces.

Hawkinge also entertained many Army and Navy top brass, and on occasions the mess resembled a combined operations headquarters. This unusual and happy state was not established through any recommendations from higher authority, but simply because the three arms of His Majesty's Services were all subjected to the same severe scrutiny from across the Channel. If we were not getting bombed from the air, some part of the coastal area could be receiving an explosive package from the German long-range coastal guns. So each service realized that none could operate successfully without the other. As far as I was aware, 'Hell Fire Corner' was the only part of Britain's island fortress where the three services forgot their differences and worked in harmony.

One evening I witnessed first-hand the true worth of our combined operations. I had been invited to dine at an army mess in Folkestone, and had hardly sat down when I was called to the phone. Hawkinge was being bombed. I sped up the hill towards the airfield, where the army was already hard at work with its searchlights and anti-aircraft guns. Away out in the Channel the Royal Navy too had obviously tangled with its opposite number in another bid for E-boat supremacy. Star shells and streams of tracer criss-crossed the sky off Dover. Further to the southeast the blackness of the night would erupt intermittently in bursts of orange fire as Bomber Command unleashed its heavy cargo of destruction upon the harbour installations at Boulogne. You could almost feel the war pulsing through your veins.

When I arrived back at Hawkinge the air raid was over, but the bright fires of many incendiaries were still burning among the tombstones in the cemetery near the main gates. It was an eerie sight—a line-up of stationary ghosts. Little damage had been done to the station itself but the enemy had scored a direct hit on my office. A lone incendiary bomb had crashed through the roof, almost above my desk, and buried itself under the floor without exploding.

January 1944 froze into February and a feeling of urgency began creeping into all areas of the south coast. One could not help noticing signs of increased activity. New landing strips, constructed and grassed during the previous summer and left vacant, were now being brought to life by skeleton staffs, all busy preparing to receive the larger components of the recently formed 2nd Tactical Air Force.

The day and night skies continually reverberated with the noise of our bombers, huge formations of Flying Fortresses of the 8th US Air Force by day, and the four-engined heavyweights of Bomber Command by night. Swarms of low-flying fighters crossed and recrossed the south coast during daylight. Light bombers, medium bombers and four-engined Lancasters and Halifaxes often limped into Hawkinge. Some were short of fuel, others, damaged by flak, were forced in by the weather and were only too thankful for a friendly place to roost.

Hawkinge was becoming more like Clapham Junction, and I began to feel I would miss the last train for the Continent if I became too deeply established in my post as station commander. It was all very comfortable and interesting, but I wanted to be part of this resurgence—this 'something in the air', this gathering of the troops, this birth of a crusade. It was all so obvious, yet so secret—one did not dare whisper the words 'Second Front'. My two Typhoon squadrons had already left Lympne; 609 Squadron moved a few miles up the coast to Manston; and No 1 Squadron had settled in at Martlesham Heath.

One morning, towards the middle of February, I had just returned to my office from the airfield when I received a telephone call from

'Ding' Saunders at group HQ. The 2nd Tactical Air Force was requesting my release from Hawkinge; it needed me to command a mobile wing of rocket-firing Typhoons. Since this would mean my eventual promotion to group captain, 'Ding' considered I would be unwise to decline. He had no need to worry. I was back in the swim again.

'Ding' was being a good friend to me. Leaving his command would have its regrets, but operationally I could never envisage 11 Group, or indeed Figher Command, competing with the rapidly expanding might of the 2nd Tactical Air Force. While the 2nd TAF was building up in support of Operation Overlord 11 Group would be reduced in squadrons to the level of an impoverished landlord.

So I took 'Ding's' advice and proceeded to the temporary HQ of 84 group at Oxford. This was also the HQ of the British Second Army, and was my introduction to the future interdependence of the tank and the aircraft. From now on the mingling of blue and khaki was to be the essence of our combined operations.

Everyone was friendly and full of enthusiasm for the mammoth task that lay ahead. My new Air Officer Commanding was Air Vice-Marshal L. O. Brown, CBE, DSC, AFC, a jovial round-faced First World War ace who, like 'Ding' Saunders, was South African. I also met several old friends, including Air Commodore Tim McEvoy, who had served on the staff at Bentley Priory, and the effervescent Fred Rosier from the Desert Air Force.

My instructions were simple. I would be forming a wing of rocket-firing Typhoons at Manston, to be known as 123 Wing 84 Group 2nd Tactical Air Force. My first two squadrons, 609 and 198, were already there, complete with their own servicing echelons. All the other ground staff, transport and Air Force paraphernalia would arrive within the next few days. It was to be completely mobile, but with everything common to a normal static air force station: doctors, hospital, field kitchens, repair and maintenance sections, armoury, equipment and signal sections.

84 Group provided me with a large V8 shooting brake, complete with my personal driver, and moving from Hawkinge to Manston was simply a matter of motoring the 30-odd miles north along the coast. Manston was near Ramsgate on a neck of land that jutted out into the channel from the northeast corner of Kent, almost directly opposite Dunkirk.

Being back at Manston was like returning to squadron life. 609 was commanded by Squadron Leader J. C. Wells, DFC, and 198 Squadron by Squadron Leader J. Baldwin, DFC and Bar. Both were old friends, both outstanding and popular leaders. Manston, like most front-line stations, was an extremely busy and happy place, As at Tangmere and Hawkinge, something was always happening, and you felt as if you were deeply involved at the business end of the air war.

Since my squadrons were to be equipped with rockets I set about making myself familiar with this new type of weapon. Obviously, much had happened since I had last served at Manston. As the great air battles raged over Germany, new and more lethal weapons were continually being developed. While teams of scientists were busy designing heavier and better bombs to rip open the already ailing heart of Hitler's Germany, others were concentrating on the development of a deadlier type of frontline firepower for the low-attack Typhoons.

The arrival of the airborne rocket was perhaps inevitable, for its basic principle was centuries old and the same as the rockets used by the Chinese against the Mongol hordes over 700 years previously. Its propellant, or 'motor', was a simple cylindrical metal tube packed with cordite. Stabilizing fins were fitted to its rear end, while at the other was attached a 60 lb streamlined warhead of metal and high explosive. When fired by an electric charge, the rocket motor set up a jet of rapidly expanding gases which forced it through the air at ever increasing velocity until the cordite charge was expended.

Eight rails were attached to the Typhoon, four under each wing, and the new rocket projectiles were slung on them parallel to the line of flight. These airborne rockets had a number of important advantages over ordinary bombs. Since they were self-propelled their velocity on impact was much greater. Also, a rocket motor created no recoil as it left its carrier, and its warhead could therefore be many times heavier and of much greater calibre than any orthodox shell that could possibly be fired from an airborne cannon.

In terms of fire power, the Typhoon was now equivalent—if not superior—to a battle cruiser. The rocket's accuracy, and the speedy manoeuvrability of its aerial platform, was superior to the performance of army artillery. So long as a reasonable degree of air superiority could be maintained, squadrons of Typhoons could patrol like sharp-eyed eagles over a wide expanse of enemy territory.

As a tactical weapon Typhoons were to change the whole concept of close-support operations. With their eight rockets and four 20 mm Hispano cannons, they would make sure that the lumbering metal giants of Hitler's prized Panzer divisions were no longer the undisputed victors of the *Blitzkrieg* days.

I received a signal that my mobile wing was in convoy and due at Manston in the late afternoon. So I motored out a few miles towards Canterbury and pulled up at the side of the road to wait for its arrival. It was not long in coming—and I could hardly believe my eyes. Headed by a line of jeeps and dispatch riders, the convoy of three-ton trucks seemed to stretch back for miles.

I saluted each component as it passed, and as the last vehicle, a flying control tender, disappeared towards Manston, I could not help thinking how vulnerable such a convoy would be if it were suddenly attacked by a squadron of rocket-firing Typhoons.

8

123 Wing, 2nd TAF

2nd Tactical Air Force was extremely fortunate in having 198 and 609 Squadrons to form the foundation for its 123 Wing. Both were outstanding low-attack squadrons and had good keen 'press on' types as their commanding officers. Both squadrons were engaged in a similar role to the one I had dictated to the Tangmere wing, so I was well versed in the daily activities of the flying side of my new appointment.

An auxiliary squadron, 609, had been formed at Yeadon, Yorkshire, during the winter of 1936, and was known as the West Riding Squadron. Its crest was typical of the county. Superimposed on a white rose were two crossed hunting horns, and on its scroll the motto 'Tally Ho'. Strangely, none of its pilots were now from Yorkshire. The majority were Belgians—tough, likeable, keen, experienced, and a great credit to their homeland. The outstanding contribution they made to the success of 609 Squadron, though often sorely won, was always a splendid example to those who flew with them.

During the comparatively brief period since it had been equipped with Typhoons, 609 had lost 25 pilots, but it had destroyed 77 enemy aircraft and many light coastal craft and railway locomotives. The squadron's previous commanding officer, Squadron Leader Pat Thornton-Brown, had been a particularly good friend not only to me but to many Typhoon pilots. While Pat and his boys had been escorting three boxes of American Marauders, he was attacked from behind by a swarm of American Thunderbolts. Recognition signals had been sent out, but the inexperienced Americans continued their attack, and shot down Pat and a Canadian pilot, 'Chuck' Miller. Both were killed.

198 was a much older squadron, recently rejuvenated. Formed in

1917 but disbanded shortly after the First World War it was not reformed again until December 1942. Like all Typhoon squadrons it suffered the usual teething troubles, but on shifting down from the north to 11 Group it quickly made a name for itself in low-level operations. The squadron's crest bore the motto *Igni Renatus* (We are reborn by fire) and pictured a phoenix holding a sword in its beak. Its pilots were cosmopolitan and much to my delight included a spattering of New Zealanders, Australians and Canadians. A tremendous—though friendly—rivalry began at Manston between 609 and 198, a rivalry that was to continue in 123 Wing until the end of the war in Europe.

For the first few days I had little time to interest myself in anything other than my mobile airfield. The sight of so much transport almost frightened me. To be effective 123 Wing, as its name implied, had to get moving, and after a number of conferences with the section commanders, many of whom had served in the Desert Air Force, we soon became familiar with the rudiments, if not some of the arts, of successful mobile air warfare. Our first major exercise was to shift from Manston to Thorney Island, a large permanent aerodrome on a small isthmus midway between Chichester and Portsmouth, some 120 miles west along the south coast.

When such a move is made the ground components of the wing are divided into two separate convoys—the forward or A party, and the rear or B party. Each must be capable of catering for and servicing the squadrons, and be independent of the other. In other words, as the A party moves forward to the new base, the B party must remain behind and service and maintain the squadrons until they are ready to fly out to the new base, where the A party should be waiting to receive them and take care of their total needs.

Before any move was made it was necessary for us to reconnoitre the new airfield. I would take forward a small party of senior section commanders, and after a thorough inspection hold a conference to decide where each component of the wing was to be situated.

To accommodate a wing under canvas was no straightforward matter and I found it necessary at times to act as mediator whenever section commanders put in strong claims for the same areas. The senior medical officer would stake out his claim for his hospital site; the catering officer for his various messes. Other sites were staked for the dispersal areas, signals, engineering, transport, repair and maintenance. All had to be fixed before the arrival of the road convoys.

My own needs were well catered for. I had a large semi-collapsible three-roomed caravan built on a six-wheel Austin truck. This monster was driven by my batman who could have it in position and ready for me within minutes of its arrival. I always had my caravan parked near the 'ops room' or briefing complex, which was staffed by both Army and Air Force intelligence officers. The centre room was my office, and the two canvas-sided extensions were used as bedrooms, one for myself and the other for visiting friends. Christened 'Leaping Lena' by my batman, it was austere but comfortable.

Once we had set out the airfield at Thorney Island, we signalled for the A party to proceed forward, and at the same time warned the convoy leader to expect surprise practice attacks by our Typhoons during the journey. This was excellent training for both pilot and ground staff. When the Typhoons buzzed the convoy all vehicles had to stop and their passengers take cover. The day after the arrival of A party I flew out in the morning to meet B party. I sighted it near Shoreham, swooped down and gave them the once over, and was agreeably surprised how quickly the personnel left their vehicles and dispersed. Had I been down there with them I would have done the same, for their entire journey lay along the coast, through an area still subject to occasional enemy fighter bomber attacks.

The wing settled into Thorney Island as if it had made the move many times before. Everything went without a hitch and without a break in our operational commitments. The squadrons were operating out of Manston on the morning of their departure and flying on the offensive from Thorney Island the same afternoon, such was the co-operation between our wings and our wheels. 164 and 183 Squadrons soon joined us. Truckload upon truckload of rocket projectiles began arriving, and as the first signs of spring began creeping into the roadside hedges I had every reason to believe we were in for a hot summer, in more ways than one.

Visitors soon arrived, some welcome, some a bloody nuisance. Now that our operational role was purely tactical we had to learn to work in harmony with our contemporaries in khaki, and although our army liaison officers proved to be good, hard-working and welcome additions to the wing, I can't say the same of some of the senior visiting Army brasshats. They were often a pain in the neck, and could well have been Hitler's gift to our wartime society. It was nearly always the one with the biggest plum in his mouth who proved the emptiest vessel, but the quickest way to flatten a pompous Army officer was to invite him to pass judgement on our standard of airfield camouflage—surrounded by so much blue, the officer in khaki could hardly refuse. Attached to the wing was a small communications flight, staffed by two pilots who spent their time running messages in flimsy two-seater Austers. These planes were light as a feather and at the least provocation would behave like one. A nod to a communications pilot was sufficient. By the time he was back on the ground his passenger was usually too pale and disorientated to give a verdict, and often left without stepping into the operations room to say goodbye.

We had been at Thorney Island for a short time only when I received a summons to a meeting at Uxbridge, No 11 Group HQ. This momentous occasion took place in the RAF cinema and I sat down surrounded by the greatest array of air force seniority I had ever seen.

It was the initial briefing by General Eisenhower on the role of the 2nd Tactical Air Force was to play in the invasion of the Continent—Operation Overlord—and as the great man took the stage accompanied by his lieutenants, Tedder, Leigh-Mallory and Coningham, there was an awesome silence. We all sensed the purpose of this historic gathering, but where was the invasion to be and when? Eisenhower's address was simple, straightforward and to the point. We would invade the Continent by way of the Normandy beaches on the morning of 5 June (later changed to the 6th).

After my Tangmere days I knew the Baie de La Seine and its Normandy beaches like the back of my hand, but as the general plan of the greatest ever combined operation slowly unfolded, the whole area took on a new dimension. The preparations were staggering: the airborne assaults, the quantity and variety of shipping, the number of army divisions, the tremendous weight of the air offensive. The scale and precision of it all made our past efforts look insignificant.

When the briefing was over there was no conversation, no laughter. No one lingered and we filed out of the cinema as though we were leaving church. Old friends appeared oblivious of each other. Expressions remained solemn. Every man seemed to feel he held the only key to the fortress of Europe, a key upon which rested the very future of our civilized society. The task ahead outweighed all our previous experiences and sent a shiver down the spine. With a mind full of doubts, hopes, fears and excitement, I climbed into my station wagon and set off for 123 Wing.

*

As the countryside blossomed into May it was not only the bees that stepped up their activity. While the Allied armies were gathering, and waiting, great battles continued to rage in the skies. Even in the dark nights of winter, between December and 24 March, Bomber Command had unleashed 20,000 heavy bombers against targets throughout Germany, including 16 major raids on Berlin. During this brief period, 1,047 British bombers were shot down, and 1,682 badly damaged.

The skies above Germany became a permanent battleground—and there was no respite. On the night of 30 March, for instance, Bomber Command sent 794 four-engined bombers to Nuremberg; 96 were shot down and many damaged beyond repair. The Eighth American Air Force, too, in spite of crippling losses, bravely fought its way into the furthest corners of the Luftwaffe's domain.

In a desperate bid to strike back, Germany gave her secret weapons, the V1 and V2, the highest priority. Flying bomb sites were constructed with feverish haste in many areas of the French coast, particularly in the Pas de Calais. So serious was this threat to London and the south coast ports that Bomber Command and the Eighth Air Force were often diverted from their strategic targets in an effort to hit these small, well-camouflaged sites. It was an expensive diversion. More than 70,000 tons of bombs were dropped on these sites and their ancillaries. A further 8,000 tons were aimed against targets connected with the long-range rocket, a total of bomb tonnage that could well have been spread on the enemy's synthetic oil, armament and aircraft industries—areas of manufacture through which flowed the life blood of Hitler's war machine.

As we were to learn later, the road to victory was badly signposted, full of potholes, and with more than one river to cross.

In the few busy weeks leading up to the invasion of the Normandy beaches, the skies throbbed incessantly with the sound of our four-engined bombers. There had been much dissension between the Chiefs of Staff as to how our heavy bombers could be best employed during the build-up to Overlord. Leigh-Mallory favoured bombing all rail and transport systems leading into the Normandy invasion area. Churchill was not in favour of this; he felt it could not be achieved without inflicting heavy casualties on the French and Belgian civilian populations.

The Commander-in-Chief of Bomber Command, Air Chief Marshal Sir Arthur Harris, preferred to continue his relentless flattening of Germany, city by city. General Spaatz of the Eight US Air Force thought that the Allied effort would be better spent against the oil plants and the enemy fighter force, particularly against airfields within operational distance of the Normandy beaches.

It was left to the Deputy Supreme Commander, Tedder, to decide. He opted for a dual solution, with the RAF heavy bombers spreading 40,000 tons of bombs on the enemy's rail transport system, while the Eighth Air Force followed suit, but also added 24,000 tons of carpet bombing on many enemy airfields.

After these attacks we learned from secret sources, as early as May, that the Germans, realising that they could no longer maintain communications between France and Germany, were on the verge of panic. Von Rundstedt, the German C-in-C West, wrote later: 'The main difficulties which arose for us at the time of the invasion were systematic preparations by your Air Forces; the smashing of the main lines of communications, particularly the railway junctions. We had prepared for various eventualities . . . that all came to nothing, or was rendered impossible by the destruction of railway communications, railway stations, marshalling yards, etc.'

In 123 Wing there was no argument about our employment in Overlord. We did as we were told. Although most of the low-attack aircraft of the TAF were still hammering away at flying bomb sites and targets of interdiction, our own orders were clear and concise— 'Destroy all enemy radar stations between Ostend and the Channel Islands'. It was a simple command, but to us who knew the strength of our opposition it was a message of death that heralded the cruellest chapter in the history of 123 Wing.

These radar installations were without doubt the most formidable targets and getting at them was like fighting your way into a hornet's nest. Most were near the coast and all held a commanding view; no matter from which direction you approached you could never surprise them, and the amount of light flak surrounding them was a true indication of their value. But with the approach of D-Day they had to be destroyed. While they remained intact it was impossible for aircraft or shipping to approach the Continent without being detected.

As our squadrons weaved their way into the strongest parts of the Atlantic wall, the radar site defences fought back like demented tigers. In attacking heavily defended ground targets there was no rule of thumb, no helpful advice to give. The experienced pilot shared the same deadly flight path as the inexperienced, and as the casualty rate mounted with the number of attacks, it became clear that our squadrons were being stripped of their backbones, those at Thorney Island losing six commanding officers in three weeks.

A classic and heroic example of one such attack was by four of our aircraft on the radar station at Cap de La Hague/Joburg on 24 May. This mission was led by Squadron Leader Niblett of 198 Squadron, who was killed a week later when attacking a similar target at Dieppe. His report read: '32 × 60 lb rockets and cannons were fired. One missing aircraft seen to crash at base of installation. Flight Sergeant Vallely crashed on target.'

A German soldier who saw this attack and was captured some months later, was so impressed that he insisted on recounting it to his interrogators:

Three Typhoons came in from the valley, flying very low. The second aircraft received a direct hit from 37 mm flak which practically shot off the tail. The pilot, however, managed to keep some sort of control and continued on straight at the target. He dived below the level of the radar structure, fired his rockets into it and then tried at the last moment to clear it. The third aircraft, in trying to avoid the damaged Typhoon, touched the latter's fuselage, and both crashed into the installation. This radar site was never again serviceable. Of the cables leading up to the target, 23 out of the 28 major leads were severed.

On the strength of our own evidence, and this German report, I later recommended the young pilot of the damaged Typhoon, Flying Officer Harold Freeman of the Royal Canadian Air Force, for a posthumous Victoria Cross, but to no avail. He had carried out many dangerous operations, and when you appreciate that any one of them could have been a major episode in the life of any soldier or sailor—or many airmen too for that matter—I considered my bitterness over this denial fully justified. As his group captain he will always remain to me Flying Officer Freeman, VC, Royal Canadian Air Force.

Squadron Leader Walter Dring, DFC, was promoted from 183 Squadron and became our new Wing Commander Flying. 'Farmer' Dring came from Spalding in Lincolnshire and was a true son of the soil. He had served in my wing at Tangmere in 1943, where his rugged exterior, wry smile and dry sense of humour had made him a great favourite with the New Zealand boys of 486 Squadron.

His promotion to be my deputy was the start of an association that was to span the hot dusty days of Normandy, the cooler though hectic days against the Channel ports, the mud of Merville, Ursel airfield in Belgium and Gilze-Rijen in flat, soggy Holland. We were to share the joys, hopes and sorrows of a modern crusade. His part in it began with a flourish, prospered, and when at its peak at the very gates of a dying Germany, ended in a crash at Chièvres in the snowbound Ardennes.

Towards the end of May, our supreme commander, General Eisenhower, and a large retinue of his staff officers, paid us a visit. The impression he made on me was a revelation. Some people you take to immediately—General Eisenhower was one of them. Most of the British generals I met during my time in England were as stiff and unbending as the silly little sticks they carried. Eisenhower's authority, humility and broad friendly smile made you feel when meeting him that you had made his day. He was well versed in the activities of our wing, and if there were aspects that were not quite clear to him, he would not leave the subject until it was fully explained.

To add interest to his visit we sent up one of our smoke carriers. Somewhere in the background, the hierarchy had thought it would be a brilliant idea if my aircraft tried even harder to gouge out the eyes of the Atlantic wall. To add to our rockets we could, when the time was ripe, lay smoke screens along the enemy beaches. Several aircraft were fitted with smoke cylinders, one under each wing. In practice, a single Typhoon flying low over the airfield could blot out the landscape and even the sun for some minutes.

As the Typhoon screamed low across the aerodrome in front of the gathered assembly nothing happened. Fortunately, three more aircraft were standing by and were immediately scrambled off in formation. They climbed, turned, and dived down towards the airfield. As they flattened out a few feet above the ground all six cylinders began streaming smoke simultaneously. It was a most impressive sight.

A permanent fixture on the station was a large flock of starlings feeding on the grass surface between the concrete runways and taxiways. Providing we kept off the grass they took no notice of our Typhoons, but the speed and density of the artificial smoke screen took them by surprise and completely overwhelmed them. They lost their horizon, became disorientated, and as we waited for the smoke to clear we had the weird sensation of scrambling and fluttering all over and around us. This amused our visitors immensely, the Supreme Commander in particular. There was hardly a breeze, and it was fully five minutes before we could move off to the operations room where Squadron Leader Wells of 609 was to give a squadron briefing.

In spite of this convincing demonstration the smoke-laying was left to the Bostons of No 2 Group. Apparently the planning staff felt, quite correctly, that our aircraft were more profitably employed in their normal role as rocket carriers.

After General Eisenhower and most of his party had left, I invited two American Air Force colonels to join Dring and myself in my caravan for drinks. I always enjoyed the company of American pilots, those from the deep South in particular. Their conversation was so refreshing; the slow southern drawl, their capacity to tell stories. They never displayed any sign of affectation, nor were their tongues ever two-edged swords. I enjoyed their cigarettes, too, even with a camel pictured on the pack.

Our Air Officer Commanding, Air Vice-Marshal 'Bingo' Brown, was a frequent visitor to the wing. As head of 84 Group he was always welcome, and normally flew himself around in a white-nosed Auster. I never asked why it was painted white, but at least it matched his hair—or what was left of it. He became very interested in a small paratrooper's motorcycle my transport officer had 'acquired' for me. This piece of army equipment put me in the top flight for mobility. I could carry it folded up in an Auster, or in a specially adapted long-range tank fitted under a wing of my Typhoon, and could be riding away on it within seconds of leaving my aircraft. This bike intrigued the old fellow immensely, and I felt that if I did not keep my eye on it it might 'disappear' in the same manner in which it had come to me.

So I was not too surprised when, arriving back from Chichester one afternoon, I came upon the Air Officer Commanding, his knees almost under his chin and his face wreathed in smiles, speeding round the airfield on my little bike. He seemed quite surprised when he saw me, and in his attempt to acknowledge my wave lost his balance, ran off the bitumen and finished up on his back on the grass verge. Hatless, and with torn trousers, he looked like an ageing Billy Bunter who had just been caught pinching some apples.

One day I had a message that Peter Fraser, the New Zealand Prime Minister, was visiting 485 Squadron at Selsey, and would like to see me. I was still smarting over the Eden affair, but I could not fob off

our Prime Minister, so I flew the few miles over to Selsey in an Auster.
Bill Jordan and Air Commodore E. G. Olson were with the Prime
Minister and after Jordan had introduced me to Fraser he gave me
a sly wink, which led me to believe our thoughts may well have
centred on the same incident.

The Prime Minister, wearing a long black coat and sombre homburg, was a man of few words; when he did speak it was almost in
a whisper, and a Scottish whisper at that. He asked if I had any New
Zealanders under my command at Thorney Island. I told him I had,
and could not help getting in a quiet dig by reminding him that the
New Zealand squadron he was at present visiting was commanded
by a Scotsman, Squadron Leader J. B. Niven, an RAF pilot from
Edinburgh. He seemed a little nonplussed at this, and I felt I had
scored a point. But being a seasoned politician my comment ran off
his back like water off a duck's, for the next thing he wanted was to
visit my wing.

The High Commissioner was anxious about time, as Mr Fraser had
to be back in London for an evening engagement with Winston
Churchill. I suggested that, if he liked to risk his neck for five minutes,
I could fly him over to Thorney Island in the Auster and Mr Jordan's
Rolls-Royce could follow by road, pick him up half an hour later,
and whisk him off to London. This agreed, the black-clad Prime
Minister was shovelled into the aircraft and we took off. It was a
warm afternoon, and the air was full of bumps, but it did not prevent
my passenger from foolishly doffing his black homburg whenever our
aircraft received the usual wave from the farm workers below.

There was quite an updraught as we crossed the bitumen perimeter
track, prior to landing on the grass near my caravan, and I put the
aircraft down in a series of kangaroo hops. After I switched off the
motor Mr Fraser remarked on the nice landing, and looked rather
puzzled when I asked him which one. We did a quick drive around
the various components of 123 Wing and, visiting my four squadrons, met most of the New Zealand pilots. As with 486 at Tangmere,
nearly all were farmers' sons and therefore cool Conservatives.

It may have been an interesting afternoon as far as Mr Fraser was
concerned, but he appeared to know little about the air war in Europe
and kept harking back to the age-old one-sided battle of the River
Plate. He became quiet when I told him about the great air battles
that raged over Germany every night. As far as our aircrew was
concerned, each battle was an El Alamein in itself. Over 600 young
airmen had been blasted from the skies in a single raid on Nuremberg.

Well over 1,000 Lancaster and Halifax bombers had been shot down
in night raids during the previous four months. And as recently as
the night of 30 March, almost 100 four-engined bombers had been
shot down. Their crews had no choice but to face the murderous skies
night after night.

I pointed out how sad it all was, particularly when the New
Zealand papers featured long lists of the casualties of their native sons
on one page, and the distressing news about the shortage of butter
and striking West Coast coal miners on the other. I think it was at
this point that I felt the second cool breath of high-level politics. The
Prime Minister froze into silence and I was rather pleased when a
smiling Bill Jordan arrived in his Rolls-Royce and took him back to
London.

9

Invasion

As the first light of a new day began stealing through the trees at the back of my caravan it was hard to believe it was 5 June. The stillness of the hour, the cool sweet scent of the morning, a cock crowing from a distant farm—all made me feel I could have been in a country churchyard. Yet tomorrow was to be D-Day.

The sharp crack of Koffman starters, followed by the bark and roar of several Typhoons, quickly brought me back to reality. Within a few minutes the entire airfield seemed to be crawling with angry Typhoons as they crabbed their way in the half light towards the end of the main runway. A red Very light arched up into the sky from the control vehicle, and the first of 40 Typhoons roared down the runway before lifting off and disappearing in the direction of the Isle of Wight. Within two or three minutes all was quiet again, except for a chirping high-pitched argument among a family of sparrows that apparently owned the tree that reached out over my caravan.

After shaving, I was joined by Squadron Leader 'Hinnie' Hines, my senior administration officer, Tom Yates, the head engineering officer, and Wing Commander Munson, who was in charge of the RAF Regiment unit that guarded our airfield. We had breakfast together, and although my secret was still intact as far as I was concerned, the impression I gained from their collective innuendoes was that they knew as much as I did about the significance of tomorrow's date.

We finished breakfast and to work off some of the tension I went up in an Auster and dropped in on a number of farmhouses near Arundel to collect several dozen eggs and a large quantity of strawberries. This buying from the black market—although highly illegal —was common practice in our wing. The farmers expected us, welcomed the cash, and kept us supplied with a variety of luxuries during our stay on Thorney Island. I enjoyed these early-morning excursions into the Sussex and Hampshire countryside and found it much easier to settle into the morning's office routine after hedgehopping around the country for half an hour or so.

5 June 1944 proceeded like most other days, until we gathered for our afternoon conference attended by all heads of sections. Although we kept these gatherings fairly informal, the atmosphere at this meeting was charged with a measure of reserve and an air of anticipation. Thus even before I began my brief address I felt I was about to tell my officers something that they already knew. I was brief and to the point. Tomorrow was simply D-Day and no ground personnel, for security reasons, must leave Thorney Island until further notice. The only comment came from Flight Lieutenant Short, our cockney transport officer: 'Cor blimey, Sir. You might 'ave warned me. I 'ad a date with a readhead in Portsmouth tonight.'

I spent the remainder of the afternoon visiting the many sections and studying the next day's flying commitments. Overlord was certainly a gigantic operation, and the war map of France in the operations caravan took on the shape and characteristics of a multi-coloured jigsaw puzzle.

In the late evening I took to the air again, this time in my Typhoon, and flew out towards the Solent. Below and as far as the eye could see was gathering the greatest armada ever to be assembled: a vast array of large, small and medium-sized ships, landing craft and naval vessels—all heading south, row upon row. It was truly a unique and momentous sight.

As I turned and flew towards the Nab tower, roughly halfway between the Isle of Wight and Selsey Bill, there was a dull red explosion as a medium-sized cargo vessel, just off Sandown, either struck a mine or stopped a torpedo. But I was too far away to see the extent of the damage, and I did not dare approach closer in case some of the gunners below were tensed up with the excitement of the hour and mistook me for an FW 190.

Returning over Thorney Island, I could see 609 and 198 below me as they prepared to land from the last mission of the day. It had been against Rommel's HQ on the Cherbourg peninsula, a highly successful strike, although we were to learn later that the old Desert Fox had left his château a few minutes before the two squadrons arrived to dismantle it.

I soon had the sky above Thorney Island to myself. With my long-kept secret now shared, I was suddenly overcome with a feeling of great relief and exaltation. I put down her nose and the Typhoon quickly gathered speed until, a few feet above the grass in front of the watch office, I eased back gently on the control column and began a wide lazy loop that took me high into the sky above our base.

It was a glorious feeling to roll off the top. From this point in the heavens I could see the vast armada to the south, and still ships by the thousand were converging on it from the east and west. Wishing them luck I started letting down in a wide gentle sweep that took me almost over Tangmere. It was practically dark as I taxied into my bay and switched off. All seemed quiet for a moment or two, but as I mounted the steps to my carvan the darkening skies began to throb again to the sound of the four-engined heavyweights of Bomber Command.

I went to bed feeling as if 5 June was the end of the beginning. I asked myself: would tomorrow be the start of yet another bloody chapter in the history of 123 Wing?

D-Day started much the same as any other—in fact it was almost an anti-climax. I nearly missed the bus, for the duties of airfield commander, the special visitors from 84 Group and 2nd TAF, the amount of trivia that seems to blossom during the most important occasions, all kept me well anchored to the ground for most of the day.

Dring and the squadrons were coming and going, extremely busy hammering away in support of the Allied landings; but in view of the confused state of the bridgehead it was almost impossible to learn exactly what was happening. Several pilots had been shot down by flak, including George Martin, a most experienced Australian. The squadrons had destroyed their first tanks in an attack on two enemy road columns. Southwest of Caen many thin-skinned vehicles had been destroyed. Until conditions on the bridgehead had stabilized, thus establishing a pronounced bombline, our activities were mainly confined to areas southeast of the main assault zone.

It was not until the evening that I was able to head for the Normandy beaches, and was just in time to join a sky train—a stream of tugs and gliders that reached out southwards from Selsey Bill as far as the eye could see. Hundreds of four-engined bombers were strung in a narrow stream, each pulling a large Hamilcar glider, all bound for the Normandy bridgehead. It was the largest glider-borne force yet to fly into battle. Most of the 6th Air Landing Brigade, including artillery and light tanks, were on their way to Normandy.

During the time I overhauled the leaders of this massive aerial armada as they passed to the west of Le Havre, and kept with them as they crossed the enemy coast near the mouth of the river Orne, not a single enemy aircraft put in an appearance. The only enemy reception was light flak in spasmodic and scattered bursts, and this was swiftly dealt with by swarms of low-attack aircraft. They were like angry bees as they worked below us, eloquent proof of our command of the air.

When the tugs began releasing their gliders I became so fascinated by the performance of these powerless wood and canvas monsters I could not take my eyes off them, and almost flew straight into a squadron of Spitfires that crossed my path on their way to Bayeux.

One glider was shot down by flak, but the rest ploughed on down into the fields alongside the Orne like a flock of exhausted black swans. Some skimmed along the ground and finished up in a cloud of yellow dust. Others hit the ground at too steep an angle and burst open like paper bags.

As the numbers mounted and the fields on the landing zone became congested, some gliders seemed to have no place to go. But they just dropped down into the smallest of spaces and elbowed their way in among the dust, splinters and torn fabric. I was surprised how quickly the tanks left their winged carriers. No sooner had one touched down than out crawled a tank like a crustacean hurriedly vacating its shell.

The German gunners were quick to size up the situation and began shelling the gliders from across the nearby Carentan Canal. Several burst into flames. I went into a steep dive towards Colombelles, hoping to catch sight of some of these German batteries, but I could see other aircraft busily engaged in straffing attacks and flew on to the southeast of Caen.

Two motorcycles and what appeared to be a staff car were racing along a road near Cagny, and I swept down and raked them with cannon fire. All three came to a sudden and dusty stop, but I did not see what became of them. A loose flight of Mustangs suddenly turned towards me and for a brief moment I mistook them for enemy fighters. By the time I had realized my mistake, and they had too, I was ringed by several streams of light flak and quickly moved myself back and out to the coast near Ouistreham.

All along the fringe of the bay, as far as visibility would permit, I could see smoke, fire and explosions. Inland some areas were completely smudged out by evil clouds of smoke. Underneath it great flashes of fire would erupt and burst like bolts of orange lightning.

Normandy was like a huge, fire-rimmed boiling cauldron. To seaward ships of all shapes and sizes lay patiently at anchor. Between them and the beaches an extraordinary regatta was taking place as hundreds of smaller craft dashed hither and thither.

I turned and flew westwards towards Bayeux, and had gone as far as St Aubin sur Mer when I was fired on by the Royal Navy. I was not too surprised; it had happened before, once over Scapa Flow in the winter of 1940 and again off Harwich in 1941. I removed myself from above the D-Day shipping, and to give the trigger-happy navy gunners a wider berth set off home by way of the enemy port of Le Havre. Further to the east the landscape was already beginning to fade into twilight. Streams of coloured tracer climbed slowly but brightly into the darkening sky away to the north of me, probably from Cap d'Antifer or Fécamp.

Like homing seabirds, many aircraft accompanied me back across the Channel. At various distances were lone Spitfires, and here and there a lumbering four-engined bomber, ragged packs of Typhoons, Mustangs and Thunderbolts, all heading for the peace and security of their home bases on the south coast of England. For us it was the end of D-Day; for many it had been the end of a lifetime. Tomorrow would be D + 1, and for our pilots more targets of interdiction.

While we in 123 Wing were sinking on to our stretchers, and the opposing armies were locked and bleeding on the Normandy bridgehead, great fleets of Allied bombers were waiting silently, primed and ready to swing another sledgehammer blow at the splintering doorway of Hitler's Europe.

By the evening of 6 June, the German Atlantic wall had been split open on a 30-mile front between the Vire and Orne rivers. The steel and concrete bastions of occupied France were pulverized and tottering, while some of our assault forces had driven wedges eight miles deep into the Normandy defences. The German air force and navy had been rendered powerless, and our rocket-firing Typhoons and fighter bombers had wrought havoc among the enemy reserves to the south and east of the invasion beaches.

It was still a shaky toehold, and one that had to withstand the pressures of the night if we were to retain the Normandy bridgehead. During daylight the enemy moved at the mercy of the skies, but once darkness spread over the land, the German armour could take to the roads and push north towards the main battle areas.

The morning of D + 1 spelt the death knell to any idea the enemy may have had for reinforcing their forward troops in daylight. All Typhoons of both 83 and 84 Groups were let loose on armed reconnaissance to the rear of the main battle. They roamed far and wide, and everything that moved, whether on rail, road or river, was strafed, rocketed or bombed.

This continuous assault from the air was a nightmare for the German General Staff. General Bayerlein, who commanded Panzer Lehr, was caught by our Typhoons between Vire and Le Bény Bocage. Later he recorded:

> Every vehicle was covered with branches of trees and moved along hedgerows and the fringes of woods ... but by the end of the day, I had lost 40 petrol wagons and 90 other trucks. Five of my tanks had been knocked out as well as 84 half-tracks, prime movers and self-propelled guns. These losses were serious for a division not yet in action

Seventeen Typhoons were shot down by flak while attacking similar targets throughout the day. Even while moving at night the enemy still felt the long arm of 123 Wing. Kurt Meyer, who commanded 12 SS Division, was ordered by von Rundstedt to hurry to Lisieux and join forces with the 21 Panzer Division, where they were to combine in dealing with any of our forces that had crossed the Orne. He set off in the late afternoon, but was so heavily attacked by our Typhoons that his column barely averaged four miles an hour. He reached Evrecy southwest of Caen by midnight, but diversions, slow running and frequent stops had almost exhausted his fuel tanks. Meyer had counted on drawing supplies from a dump near Evrecy, but on arriving in the small hours of the morning he found nothing but a mountain of blackened and smoking drums. 609 Squadron had beaten him to it.

Much has been written about the thrusts, counter-thrusts and controversies of those early days in Normandy. But as an airman I must here speak up on behalf of all members of 123 Wing—indeed of every branch of the Allied Air Force. Their role has been consistently understated.

Back in 1942, the buildup of the Desert Air Force under Air Marshal Coningham had lifted General Montgomery above the level of his unfortunate predecessors and placed him on the pedestal of public popularity. The press headlines were always 'Monty Strikes

Again', 'Monty's Victory', 'Monty's Army'. The Desert Air Force, Tedder or Coningham were seldom mentioned.

Montgomery appeared to revel in this idolization and carried his opinions across the beaches and into the bomb-scarred fields of Normandy. His declaration—'I would sooner use a thousand shells than lose one single life'— was well received by his troops, and in their eyes he became a god of war who could do no wrong.

But the view that aircraft and their pilots were expendable, mere weapons of convenience, rang a discordant note in the ears of all of those who flew. The fact that our air supremacy went unchallenged in the initial first 48 hours was in no way to Montgomery's credit. Without air supremacy the invasion could never have been attempted, and undoubtedly our command of the air was the most important single factor in the success of the invasion. Without Coastal Command the seas would still have been alive with U-boats. Without Bomber Command and the Eighth Air Force the great industrial cities of Germany would still have been churning out weapons in ever-increasing quantities.

Our strategic bombing had had a profound psychological effect on Germany's civilian population. The Tactical Air Force, rocket-firing Typhoons and fighter bombers, maintained a successful interdiction of the Seine bridges and ensured victory in the land battles before they had even begun, crippling the enemy's armour as it lay waiting in the hedgerows.

It was the day of the eagle, yet it was General Montgomery who accepted the accolade.

As far as 2nd TAF was concerned, every day was a day of maximum effort. Field-Marshal Rommel summed up the situation in Normandy, when on 12 June (D + 6) he sent this teleprinter signal to Field-Marshal Keitel, Chief of the Wehrmacht Supreme Command:

The enemy is strengthening himself visibly on land, under cover of very strong aircraft formations. Our own operations are rendered extraordinarily difficult, and in part impossible to carry out. The enemy has complete command of the air over the battle zone, and up to about 100 kilometres behind the front, and cuts off by day almost all traffic on the roads or byways, or in open country. Troops and staffs have to hide by day, in areas which afford some cover ... Neither our flak, nor the Luftwaffe seem capable of putting a stop to this crippling and destructive operation of the enemy's aircraft.

As each day passed the Allied armies dug their feet deeper into the soil of Normandy. Unless Hitler could provide something extra special our tenure of the bridgehead seemed secure. In desperation the German High Command set upon London with the first of their secret weapons— the V1 or flying bomb. Had these assaults begun six months earlier, as intended, they could well have disrupted all our invasion plans. Thanks to Bomber Command, and its raid on the German experimental station at Peenemünde as early as August 1943, both the V1 and V2 rockets arrived on the scene much behind schedule.

However, by 12 June some 12,000 flying bombs were produced and ready to be launched against London and the south coast ports. These were stored well away from the prying eyes of the RAF in dumps spread over Germany, France and Belgium. But to their cost the Germans again failed to appreciate the flexibility of the RAF. They had counted on shifting these bombs to their firing points along the French coast by rail, but attacks by the RAF made this very difficult. Rail bridges, junctions, marshalling yards and locomotives had already been effectively dealt with; heavy and concentrated attacks on flying bomb launching sites added to the confusion.

Through our secret service we had also learned the locations of some of the enemy's storage areas. One of these dumps was in a large underground system of tunnels in the Oise valley at St Leu-d'Esserent. It held an estimated 2,000 flying bombs. Bomber Command smashed in the roof of these tunnels using the heaviest bombs, and imprisoned the flying bombs where the French had once grown their mushrooms. Another dump, holding 1,000 V1s, was smashed by American bombers.

These attacks on Hitler's secret weapons were not achieved without loss. Two thousand aircrew lost their lives in what might be described as the second Battle of Britain.

Hitler had hoped to open his assault on London by firing off his new weapons in salvos, 64 at a time. The best he could do on the first night—12 June—was to dispatch 10 bombs, only one of which reached the London area. Nevertheless in the weeks that followed the Londoners had to brave further assaults from the sky. The arrival of these 'doodlebugs' had a sizeable effect on our own invasion efforts. Many Bomber and Fighter Command formations were taken from their tactical and strategic commitments to wage a separate war against this new weapon.

On 14 June some of 123 Wing's squadrons landed in France for the first time. Several airfields had been hurriedly prepared by the airfield construction companies, and, although some were still shelled from time to time, the fact that we could refuel, and seek the safety of a comparatively nearby Normandy runway if in trouble, was a tremendous stride forward and a great boost to morale.

However, our squadrons had sustained severe losses in the build-up to D-Day and the operations that followed, and I was becoming increasingly worried about the quality and lack of experience of replacement air crew. Some of the old hands had survived, but we had lost too many squadron and flight commanders. Many of the boys, who in most cases had come straight from their operational training units, did not survive their first mission. While we were still based in England we could add to their experience with a period of intensive training, but once we were established on the overcrowded bridgehead this was quite out of the question. A new boy's first flight had to be operational.

Hurn airfield, near Bournemouth, was our final assembly area before the ground components of 123 Wing left by sea for Normandy. Hurn was barely 35 miles to the west of Thorney Island, and to give the wing a chance for a further 'shake-down', we spent a few days at Funtingdon airfield before moving on to Hurn. Our squadrons were attached to an 83 Group Wing at B10, which was near Plumetot, four miles north of enemy-occupied Caen. During this period of enforced separation from our squadrons, I did my best to spend part of each day at either end of my stretched-out command. With the squadrons in Normandy and the ground components at Hurn, it was not always easy.

B10, like some of the other hurriedly constructed airfields, was still repeatedly shelled and this dusty airstrip was a most uncomfortable place to live. Trying to sleep at B10 was an experience in itself. Prior to arriving in Normandy my bed had been separated from the German army by the width of the Channel. At B10 only four miles of open country lay between us, and at night the thunder of the guns was terrific. A number of our own heavy army guns were dug into the edge of the airstrip near to where we slept in slit trenches. When they fired they almost seemed to lift you out of your trench, and the answering German 88s often rattled shrapnel on to the iron sheet that covered my narrow grave-like sleeping place.

Cam Malfroy, New Zealand's prewar Davis Cup player, accompanied me over to B10 one afternoon. After nightfall we were walking towards our slit trenches before settling in when Cam decided he wanted a cigarette. No sooner had he struck a match than a spurt of dirt hit my trouser leg and a bullet ricocheted off into the darkness. Some sharp-eyed sniper had fired at us, and had his aim been a little higher, and to the right, he might well have flattened me. To be shot down out of the skies was bad enough, but to be bowled over on the ground by a member of the Wehrmacht, and at night too, was unthinkable.

Martraghy, or B7 as it was known, was to be the home of 123 Wing during its time in Normandy. It lay a few miles south of Bayeux and was a much better airfield than B10, and a good deal safer too. After the wing had arrived by sea we set up our administration quarters, operations room and various messes in a large orchard on the western edge of the airfield. Apart from the cover afforded by the apple and pear trees, a high hawthorn hedge surrounded the perimeter of this rather pleasant place, and it was far enough from the airstrip to escape most of the dust.

We ran into serious trouble with our Typhoons almost as soon as they began operating from Normandy soil. In the pre-invasion period our secret agents had kept us well informed about many aspects of the invasion area, but there was one serious problem we had not foreseen: the Normandy dust contained a hard silicon-like material that cut into the 24 cylinders of our sleeve-valve motors like abrasive emery powder.

Our airstrip was built in what had been a wheat field. We had bulldozed off the topsoil down to a good hard layer of clay and covered that with heavy wire meshing. This gave a solid base to fly from, but it did not stop the dust. When our Typhoons took off they sucked it into their huge air scoops with disastrous results. It could wear a motor out in fewer than 10 hours flying time, and special filters had to be hurriedly designed, manufactured and fitted to all Typhoons. It was a worrying time for our engineering staff, particularly Tom Yates, our senior engineering officer, who lost many hours of sleep before all our aircraft were modified.

Once we had settled in at B7 we were able to adapt ourselves to the real essence of close-support operations. By 1 July the Americans on the right flank had silenced all opposition on the Cherbourg peninsula and had taken some 40,000 prisoners. It was a different story in Montgomery's area on the left flank. 123 Wing were wedded to the support of the Canadians and those British units assigned to the task of rolling up the Channel ports on their way to the Rhine. Caen became a stumbling-block, and in this torrid section of the bridgehead, the war had almost taken the shape of some of the battles of the First World War. In some areas near Caen the opposing forces were facing each other across narrow strips of no-man's-land.

During this period I was frequently at the front line observing at first hand how our Typhoons were attending to the army's requirements. One evening, while I was talking to a British army captain in charge of a heavy field gun, four Typhoons dropped out of the sky, flew through a hail of flak, and fired their rockets at a target about half a mile ahead of us. I asked the captain what the Typhoons were attacking. He replied that they were 88 mm guns. I asked why he was not using some of his own shells on them, and he unashamedly answered: 'Oh, quite simple. If we fire at them, they fire back at us and we have to shift our gun again!' I must say I met few army officers who thought along those lines. Even if Normandy was their first taste of battle, most made up for lack of experience with great tenacity and courage.

A few evenings later I was accidentally and unexpectedly caught up in a real soldiers' war near some crossroads to the north-west of Caen, and it scared the living daylights out of me. I had passed through the road barrier, proceeded towards the front line, and left my jeep to join up with a party of infantrymen making their way towards an avenue of poplar trees that almost hid the road running out to the right of us. We spread out across a field containing a number of wrecked tanks and many German dead. I thought that the Germans, all with their pockets turned inside out, were probably members of the Hitler Youth. They looked like wax dolls, spread-eagled on the ground or curled up like sleeping children. With their uniforms and boots far too big for them and their short silken hair, they looked as if they belonged in the classroom. The haunting sweet smell of death hung heavily in the air and reminded me of Christmas lilies and quiet churchyards.

I was about to say something to a young lieutenant when hell and disruption broke loose as Spandaus and mortar began firing from the other side of the avenue ahead of us. I did not know whether to fall flat on my face or turn and run. The lieutenant grabbed me by the sleeve and we sprinted the 20 to 30 yards to the shelter of the poplars.

I dived behind the nearest trunk, but it was not wide enough to cover the width of my shoulders, and so I lay on my side. The lieutenant was behind a tree six or seven yards to the right of me. Mortars were exploding in the field we had just walked over and bullets were whining off the branches above us. With my heart in my throat I was thinking 'What a bloody way to die!' The young officer was shouting orders to his troops, and several grenades exploded on the other side of the road. These were quickly followed by rapid rifle fire. The din ceased as suddenly as it had begun, but like my nearby companion I remained frozen to the ground.

After a period of silence, and with my face buried in the grass, I looked across at the lieutenant to find him surrounded by several of his troops. My knees were trembling so much I had to hoist myself up by way of the tree trunk. I could see immediately all was not well. The lieutenant was dead, a bullet having ripped open the side of his head.

This sudden and violent enemy outburst was the work of four or five young and very brave Germans. During the morning's battle they must have hidden in the rubble of some bombed-out buildings at the road junction. After the battle had passed by they had returned to their one-man foxholes on the other side of the built-up roadway and from this position tried to drive us off. Outnumbered 30-to-1 they must have accepted the inevitable and decided to die for their Fatherland. No other British troops were killed, although some needed medical attention.

On the road, near where this brave little band had stood in their foxholes for the last time, lay a German youth who had literally been ironed out earlier in the day by passing tanks. His uniformed body was spread out like a sheet of grey cardboard, and his completely severed head lay face up on the dusty grass verge, its blond hair spattered with dried blood. I bent down to shift it further from the roadway, and was staggered by its weight.

It was a warm evening, yet the sweat was cold upon my brow. The rumble of the distant guns grew louder and several aircraft swept low above my head. They could have been friend or foe. It did not seem to matter.

With the Caen sector relatively stable and our squadrons well settled in at B7, we were able to set about the enemy in detail. We began operating in 'cab rank'. A squadron or squadrons would patrol over the front line and be directed on to targets by a system of ground control known as Visual Control Point (VCP). Experienced RAF officers attached to forward army formations rode in tanks or reconnaissance vehicles fitted with VHF radios tuned to our own frequency. Working with the same gridded maps as our own, these officers could tell us which targets the army wanted us to attack. If a self-propelled gun in a certain grid number was giving trouble we would immediately streak down and blow it to pieces. Tanks, guns, mortar positions and troop concentrations were attacked in this manner, some very close to our own troops. It was the ultimate in close-support operations.

In spite of this harassment of the perimeter of Caen, Montgomery seemed to be making little headway. This caused much dissension in high Army and RAF circles anxious to get control of the enemy airfields to the southwest, particularly Caen-Carpiquet. Montgomery again asked for the support of Bomber Command, and as usual his request was granted.

Nearly 500 Lancaster and Halifax bombers dropped 2,500 tons of bombs on the northern outskirts of Caen in the early evening of 7 July. It was a tremendous spectacle, but as at Cassino it was so thorough that it defeated its purpose. The approaches to the city centre were blocked off by mountains of rubble and stone and our assault troops could barely find their way in. To me it all seemed so unnecessary, but I ensured that our Typhoons did everything that was asked of them—and often a great deal more.

When we arrived in Normandy we worked mainly to a pattern set by 84 Group operations control. Early-morning reconnaissance patrols sighting enemy road convoys would report to group operations, who would dictate to me the number of squadrons I should dispatch. This system backfired once or twice, and so I decided to do away with the middle man—Group HQ. When the reconnaissance squadron took off at first light the others would stand by on cockpit readiness to scramble off at a moment's notice. When the reconnaissance squadron sighted a road convoy it radioed immediately to our own operations room stating the nature of their find and the size of the required reinforcements—one, two or even three squadrons. One squadron would attack the column and remain until the next arrived.

This method kept the convoy stationary, its drivers and tank crews hiding in the ditches or other handy cover. This meant that no convoy could disperse into the orchards and woods that covered large areas of Normandy. From the first sighting, Typhoons would attack continuously until the whole column was aflame from end to end. The old system allowed a break in our attention, and by the time the next squadron arrived the enemy would be dispersed out of sight in the woods.

It was a very successful departure from orthodoxy, and was to stand us in good stead at various times later in the campaign, particularly when Group HQ were changing their position while trying to keep up with the advance. It was like conducting our own private war. The pilots appreciated this extra licence, and set about their operational tasks like well-trained aerial battalions. There was always a great spirit of rivalry among the squadrons, but, when necessary, the four would combine as one.

My main concern at this stage was the shortage of suitable replacement pilots. Sending inexperienced young men to Normandy was fair neither on them nor on the experienced pilots who had to lead them. After I explained my fears to our Group AOC, 2nd TAF circularized all Spitfire squadrons asking for volunteers. Those pilots who did accept would return to England and complete a conversion course at our Group support unit at Lasham before being posted back to a Typhoon squadron.

The response was most disappointing. Not a single Spitfire pilot applied. So it was necessary to withdraw them, even if unwillingly, from their respective squadrons, which was not the happiest of situations. Few took kindly to their new role, and some even unashamedly illustrated their anxiety when interviewed either by myself or Wing Commander Dring. Others philosophically accepted their transfer to rocket-firing Typhoons and acquitted themselves well in the weeks that followed.

10
Falaise

One morning, when the Normandy sky was still tinged with red, our Typhoons roared off the dusty airstrip and swung low over the pockmarked landscape east of Bayeux. The dark shapes of many ships stood off to seaward, and near the beaches smaller craft whitened the dark surface of the sea in frenzied streaks and crosses.

Swirling clouds of yellow dust hung above the busy roads beneath us, and further to the southeast the battered city of Caen flickered and smouldered under a huge mushroom of pink and black smoke. Southwards, in the region of Villers Bocage, a furious gun battle was taking place, and to the west, thin streams of coloured tracer spouted into the morning sky before falling away in chains of red-hot clusters.

Across the river Orne the dark forest of Bretteville stretched out before us, and moments later we were brushing the tree tops as we raced on in the direction of Falaise. In the more open country the fields were strewn with the bloated carcasses of hundreds of tan and white cattle. Shell craters, bomb-holes and burnt-out tanks littered the tortured countryside.

To the south of Potigny we began climbing but streams of light flak came racing up towards us. So I hastily sank down again to the comparative safety of the taller trees and hedgerows. No sooner had we crossed the railway to the north-west of Falaise when I caught sight of the object of our early-morning mission. The road was crammed with enemy vehicles—tanks, trucks, half-tracks, even horse-drawn wagons and ambulances, nose to tail, all pressing forward in a frantic bid to reach cover before the skies once more became alive with the winged death of the 2nd Tactical Air Force.

As I sped to the head of this mile-long column, hundreds of German troops began spilling out into the road to sprint for the open fields and hedgerows. I zoomed up sharply over a ploughed field where 20 or 30 Germans in close array were running hard for a clump of trees. They were promptly scythed down in spurts of dust by a lone Mustang which appeared from nowhere.

The convoy's lead vehicle was a large half-track. In my haste to cripple it and seal off the road, I let fly with all eight rockets in a single salvo; I missed but hit the truck that was following. It was thrown into the air along with several bodies, and fell back on its side. Two other trucks in close attendance piled into it. There was no escape. Typhoons were already attacking in deadly swoops at the other end of the column, and within seconds the whole stretch of road was bursting and blazing under streams of rocket and cannon fire. Ammunition wagons exploded like multi-coloured volcanoes. A large long-barrelled tank standing in a field just off the road was hit by a rocket and overturned into a ditch. Several teams of horses stampeded and careered wildly across the fields, dragging their broken wagons behind them. Others fell in tangled, kicking heaps, or were caught up in the fences and hedges.

It was an awesome sight: flames, smoke, bursting rockets and showers of coloured tracer—an army in retreat, trapped and without air protection. The once proud ranks of Hitler's Third Reich were being massacred from the Normandy skies by the relentless and devastating fire power of our rocket-firing Typhoons.

We continued to hammer away in support of Montgomery's armies, particularly in their bid for Caen. Rommel was an astute and tough opponent and his troops fought for every inch of ground. Caen held the padlock to the gate which kept us on the Normandy bridgehead, and the longer the enemy successfully defended it, the greater the dissension grew in the Allied Supreme Command.

Again Bomber Command was called in. For three hours after dawn on the morning of 18 July the heaviest and most concentrated air attack yet made in support of ground forces flew into action, the land between Caen and Troarn being pulverized by 8,000 tons of high explosive.

It all seemed so ridiculous. Bomber Command was a strategic weapon of great importance, yet it was directed wastefully away from its primary objectives. It was like trying to kill a canary by attacking its cage with a long-handled shovel. The occupant had little chance of escape, but his friends on the outside only felt the breeze. The areas on the flank were untouched, and the Germans replied to the British assault troops with their 88 mm guns and Panther and Tiger tanks. All three could outshoot the British 25-pounders, so it was left to the fighter bombers and our rocket-firing Typhoons to take over where Bomber Command left off.

The biggest blow to the Germans came on the night of 17 July near the small village of Ste Foy de Montgommery. Rommel was attacked by Typhoons while travelling in his staff car after inspecting his defence positions. His driver was blasted from behind the wheel and the car crashed into a tree, hurling Rommel on to the road and gravely injuring him.

The long-drawn-out battle for Caen came to a close on 20 July, but the German forces were far from finished in the areas to the south-east of Caen and on the northern side of the Orne river.

As Caen fell, so did I—but not out of the sky. Squadron Leader Paul Ezanno, the bravest Frenchman I ever knew, who was commanding 198 Squadron, arrived back on the wing after being shot down by flak. Most boys who survived a bale-out or crash-landing returned to the wing as guests of the army, sometimes in jeeps, sometimes in ambulances. Not Paul. He arrived mounted on a magnificent liver-coloured thoroughbred stallion, complete with ornate saddle and bridle. Normandy was well known for its thoroughbred industry and it could well have belonged to one of its many studs. I noticed that it had recently been shod, so no doubt it had been commandeered by the Germans before Paul 'captured' it.

Paul rode up to my caravan, dismounted, and like Sir Walter Raleigh, bowed low and invited me to climb aboard. Accepting his offer I cantered out on to the clay road surrounding the airfield. Halfway round I gave my mount his head and we were soon moving along at a fast gallop. I had driven around the road plenty of times before, and knew that a mesh taxiway crossed the road on the northern side of the airstrip. In a car, truck or jeep you just motored over it. But a horse has iron shoes and although I had ridden horses since I was a child, it did not register with me until too late that iron against iron could be a slippery combination.

I did not have time to rein him in, so I tried to pull him to the left, but we were travelling far too fast. He galloped on to the wire mesh at an angle, and as soon as his feet touched, his legs slid from under him and he crashed on top of me.

I regained consciousness with the padre leaning over me. I was fighting to get my breath and he kept trying to drown me by pouring water down my throat. The horse, whinnying signals of distress, was standing almost over me, blood squirting from a large gash on his near elbow.

On my way to hospital in one of our ambulances, I told Squadron Leader G. L. Gryspeerdt, my senior doctor, who was at my side, that the bloody ambulance had square wheels. I kept drifting in and out of cloud, but remembered being put on the operating table, having my clothes cut off, and thinking 'What a bloody awful end to my invasion efforts'. I recognized Group Captain Fred Rosier (now Air Marshal Sir Fred Rosier) from 84 Group, but he soon disappeared with everything else when the hypodermic needle sank into my arm.

Next day I woke up in an RAF field hospital. My right leg, ankle and kneecap were broken, and the flesh above my knee joint was torn to the bone. I had my own private ward—a 12 feet-square tent attached to the side of a large marquee which contained the main hospital ward. For the first few days I was totally bewildered. My leg could not be plastered because my knee rose up like a ruptured pumpkin, and I was put on a special drug which temporarily sent me blind. The doctors considered having me flown back to England, but the senior doctor thought it would be unwise.

Apparently the Normandy soil carried a breed of microbe which our secret agents had failed to detect, and I became very sick. A specialist was flown over from England, bringing with him a supply of the new wonder drug, penicillin. Squadron Leader McKay undoubtedly saved my leg, if not my life. For almost a week he did not leave my side, and between my penicillin injections would sit near my bed reading to me from the Bible. Once the swelling subsided and I could be stitched up, my leg was encased in plaster from the sole of my foot to the top of my thigh.

Lying in a tented hospital had its moments. 'Bingo' Brown was a frequent visitor, and I owe much to him for my rapid recovery, but canvas is a poor substitute for bricks and mortar, and the childlike whimperings and short sharp screams from my fellow wounded filtered through the canvas or pierced the walls. I preferred the night hours, with the thunder of our anti-aircraft guns and the drone of the enemy bombers. The noise would take my mind off the smell of antiseptic and the murmurings of the dying. Sometimes fragments of flak would fall on the tent and cut peepholes to the stars. When things got really noisy above us, I would cover my face with my steel helmet and put my arms under the metal cradle that covered my legs.

One day, when I was lying looking out through the open tent flap, there was a tremendous explosion only about a hundred yards away as a Typhoon dived straight down under full power and buried itself in the ground. I never found out which wing it belonged to but Dring informed me it was not from one of our squadrons.

Once on the mend I could have been flown back to England and lost my command. I am sure my AOC was aware that this would have broken me and so after a little less than three weeks in hospital I was back in my caravan and under the attention of our own medical staff. 'Farmer' Dring had filled my shoes as airfield commander and kept me well informed on the activities of the wing, and I was soon making my way round the airfield on crutches. Tom Yates even fitted a special cradle to the side of my jeep to hold my plastered leg, so I could drive myself round.

No sooner had I settled in back at B7 when an outbreak of dysentery hit the bridgehead. It was bad enough for those on the ground. For those who took to the air it was acutely uncomfortable and embarrassing. Pulling out of dives when attacking ground targets always forced the blood away from your brain, and momentarily gave you the impression that you were flying through a cloud of star-studded spider webs. Unfortunately, it also put great pressure on your lower bowel, and I had to send a plane over to England to pick up a large supply of extra underpants to distribute among my pilots. Dysentery is a painful complaint and I was relieved when our medical staff found a cure.

During the first week in August the Germans prepared to launch a counterattack in the area of Mortain, aiming to force their way to the coast at Avranches and cut off the Americans under General Patton—who had reached Le Mans. Their preparations could not be hidden from our reconnaissance planes, and the Allies regarded the threat most seriously. While American Mustangs and Thunderbolts descended on enemy communications and transport behind the forward areas, the rocket-firing Typhoons took on the German armour. By mid-afternoon on 7 August any idea the Germans may have had of reaching Avranches was blown sky high in the vicinity of Mortain.

It had been a bold move on the part of the enemy, but its defeat spelt the beginning of the end of the German occupation of Normandy. It also proved conclusively that major ground offensives can be defeated by the use of tactical air power alone. Von Kluge wrote after the war: 'The armoured operation was completely wrecked exclusively by the Allied Air Forces, supported by a highly trained ground wireless organization.' 123 Wing rocket-firing Typhoons alone attacked 87 tanks on the afternoon of 7 August.

The aerial thrashing the enemy suffered at Mortain must have numbed the senses of the German General Staff. With the Canadians and British forcing their way south towards Falaise, and the American Third Army driving north towards Argentan, a great steel net was being thrown around the whole of the German Seventh Army. Even as late as 9 August von Kluge, in blind obedience to the Führer's orders, continued to pour troops into the closing trap. However, it was not until 11 August that he realized the nature and seriousness of this Allied threat and began frantically to withdraw towards the Seine. But it was too late and the gigantic net was rapidly closing. By the evening of the 12 August, the 2nd TAF were launching an all-out effort to close it off completely. The withering, terrifying power of our fighter bombers and rocket Typhoons began scorching the battle area with methodical ferocity.

General Bayerlein's report of 13 August described only the prelude to what was to follow during the days leading up to 30 August, when we began crossing the Seine: 'They swept in low over at least 250 motor transport, trucks, cannon and Nebelwerfer, on the roads in and around the village, and in nearby fields and orchards. They hit a truck train of rocket ammunition right off the bat, and this started exploding and throwing rockets in all directions. The streets were so littered with burning autos, trucks and other equipment, they became impassable.'.

The German Seventh Army, aided by divisions from the north, fought desperately, but low-attack squadrons ripped into their armour, and the greatest German defeat since Stalingrad began. Enemy transport that had previously run the gauntlet in spasmodic haste and opportunist caution threw discretion to the winds and began to press and jostle eastward in a growing stream. It was a retreat of the worst order as the escape route became choked with thousands of vehicles—tanks, half-tracks, petrol and ammunition wagons and horse-drawn transport. From the air it looked like the death throes of a panic-stricken and broken Juggernaut.

The Falaise pocket—as it was to be known—became the chopping block and the graveyard of Hitler's Seventh Army. The divisions sent from the north to reinforce it were also systematically torn to shreds and as I hobbled around my wing on crutches, Dring and the squadrons blasted their way through blazing hot days of maximum activity. The Falaise Gap was closed on 20 August, but elements of armoured formations outside the pocket, aided by co-ordinated action by similar formations inside, tried desperately to force it open again. This situation was causing our armies some concern, and 123 Wing were called in to tidy up. It proved to be one of the finest close-support operations in the history of 84 Group, and is best described by its own historian:

> The Army asked the RAF whether they could deal with it. It was a tricky problem. The area was small, not too easy to find, and above all the distance between the Canadian and Polish Units operating on each side of it was also very small. However, it was a vitally necessary operation and four squadrons of R/P Typhoons of 123 Wing (183, 198, 609 and 164 squadrons) led by W/C W Dring DFC (since deceased) went out to attack with the aid of VCP control. Careful briefing, good control, excellent leadership and accurate firing combined to make the operation a brilliant success. W/C Dring was awarded an immediate DSO and a conservative claim was 13 tanks destroyed and 7 damaged. As is well known, the jaws of the trap remained firmly closed.

For the Germans it was a catastrophe. Many had earlier escaped the trap and fled for the Seine, but they left behind 1,300 tanks, 1,500 field guns, 20,000 vehicles and 400,000 troops, half of whom were taken prisoner. Those troops who escaped this holocaust still had to cross the Seine. With the few bridges either in Allied hands or out of reach of the enemy troops, it was another nightmare for the remnants of a once proud army. They could either swim or take their chances on the few barges and ferries that remained afloat.

It was while attacking these river targets that we lost four aircraft of 183 Squadron—all shot down by Me 109s. This was unexpected since we had seen little of the German air force in Normandy. Their planes were normally smacked down as soon as they left their bases by the Spitfires, Mustangs and Thunderbolts which continually roamed deep into enemy territory.

During the days that covered the Falaise battle and the German retreat across the Seine, our wing entertained a number of VIPs. Senior service officers such as Air Marshal Leigh-Mallory, or Tedder, were no problem, for they understood the functions of the wing; but civilian strangers from across the Channel could prove quite a trial.

One day a party of parliamentarians arrived, headed by Colonel

Clifton-Brown, Speaker of the House of Commons. Our Continental activities and our lifestyle at B7 were a far cry from Westminster and with their many and often amusing questions the visitors reminded me of a bunch of kids who had suddenly been let loose in a zoo. First one and then another of the party would sidle up to me and in a half whisper enquire when I had been shot down. Telling them that I had been forced out of my cockpit by a horse produced varied reactions. Some peered over their glasses in disbelief, others looked elsewhere for more dramatic news. None asked about the health of the horse.

Colonel Clifton-Brown, a First World War veteran, was quite the nicest of men, but I caught him furtively secreting two 20 mm high explosive cannon shells into his coat pocket. I tapped him on the shoulder, shook my head, and pointed under the wing of a Typhoon to the steel case which had previously contained them. He blushed and appeared completely lost for words but on his return to the House of Commons he wrote me a charming and quite touching letter which showed no sign of his having been offended.

Dust, dry rations, drama and dysentery—such was life on the bridgehead, and I longed for a hot bath. So as soon as our visitors had gone I lowered myself into the cockpit of my Typhoon. With my leg in plaster this was not easy, particularly as my right foot was far too fat for its stirrup, but I soon roared off the strip in a cloud of dust and began making my way across the 80 miles of sea to Tangmere.

While working hard on my stirrups during take-off my plaster-covered foot had become firmly wedged in and I was unable to withdraw it. This did not worry me unduly until just off Le Havre, when three Thunderbolts flying towards Normandy suddenly whipped around and began taking a lively interest in me. Remembering what had happened to Pat Thornton-Brown's Typhoon, I tried to pull my foot free and began frantically waggling my wings. For a few moments I had visions of being shot down and not being able to bale out, but the American Thunderbolt pilots eventually realized their error and I was greatly relieved when we continued on our respective ways.

Paddy met me at the Tangmere watchtower and I was helped out of my cockpit by some ground staff boys before being driven off to station sick quarters. The nursing staff rigged up an apparatus to keep the plastered leg above water, and Normandy could have been on the other side of the world as I lay back in steaming luxury for a full half hour.

Paddy would not let me return to the bridgehead that evening and

I spent an enjoyable time drinking and talking with him and Air Marshal Sir Keith Park, who was also staying the night. I had never met my fellow New Zealander before, and I was most impressed by his sincerity and quiet, almost Victorian, charm. Keith Park may well have been the victor in the Battle of Britain; he could well have felt the sharp knives that followed his victory; but at no time did he mention either. He even spoke kindly of Leigh-Mallory, and I greatly admired him for that. Unlike many officers of air rank, I believe Air Marshal Keith Park would have made a fine bishop.

After a hearty breakfast of bacon and eggs I flew back to Normandy and was soon down amongst the dust. To keep well clear of the Royal Navy I had crossed back just north of Trouville. Eastward, in the direction of Rouen, the army and air force were hard at work and great columns of smoke from the winding Seine reached high into the morning sky.

During the afternoon I took several of my pilots for a drive to the area around Falaise. The scene was hard to believe as we surveyed the frayed and tattered remnants of a defeated army. The roads were choked with wreckage and the swollen bodies of men and horses. Bits of uniform were plastered to shattered tanks and trucks and human remains hung in grotesque shapes on the blackened hedgerows. Corpses lay in pools of dried blood, staring into space and as if their eyes were being forced from their sockets. Two grey-clad bodies, both minus their legs, leaned against a clay bank as if in prayer.

I stumbled over a typewriter. Paper was scattered around where several mailbags had exploded. I picked up a photograph of a smiling young German recruit standing between his parents, two solemn peasants who stared back at me in accusation. Suddenly I realized for the first time that each grey-clad body was a mother's son. The snapshot slipped through my fingers and fluttered away with the unwelcome thoughts.

Although the roads and byways around Falaise were full of tragic and horrifying sights, strangely enough it was the fate of the horses that upset me most. Harnessed as they were, it had been impossible for them to escape, and they lay dead in tangled heaps, their large wide eyes crying out to me in anguish. It was a sight that pierced the soul, and I felt as if my heart would burst. We did not linger but hurried back to the sanctity of our busy airfield near Bayeux.

The people of Normandy made a cheese that looked like over-ripe custard—unlike our own solid New Zealand cheddar. It was packed in tiny round wooden boxes and on first acquaintance seemed most definitely of the 'two-handed' variety, which you ate with one hand and held your nose with the other. But it had a pleasant taste, and like most of the other New Zealanders on 123 Wing I became rather fond of it.

While beer was unavailable, champagne became the most popular drink in the world. Once the Germans were driven homewards across the Seine, champagne—in green bottles that popped, fizzed and sparkled—began arriving at B7 by the 3-ton truckload. The first few glasses tickled your nose, and by the time you had emptied a bottle you felt like the King of Siam. But the next day your mouth felt like the bottom of a parrot's cage and your head thumped like a steam hammer.

But the British love their beer, so we started running what we called a 'shufti-kite' across to Shoreham, where a local brewery would fill two 90-gallon jettison tanks attached below each wing of a Typhoon. Then the pilot would hurry back across the Channel to B7 and we would drink the beer quickly. On the trip over to Normandy it took on a rather metallic taste, but the wing made short work of it.

This arrangement came to a sudden halt when our aerial brewer's dray was attacked by American Thunderbolts twice in one day and was forced to jettison its beer tanks into the Channel. Unlike the champagne, beer cost us money, and these two encounters proved expensive.

The young Americans, who arrived late in the European war to fly the fat-bellied Thunderbolts, were full of enthusiam but far too impulsive. Teaching them aircraft recognition was pointless as they would chase anything that flew—their own aircraft included. Low down and without attachments, a Typhoon would shoot the pants off a Thunderbolt, but we had to make allowances for our American allies and turn the other cheek.

After the supply of beer was halted, I had cases of Guinness flown over in an old twin-engined Anson. The troops mixed it with champagne to produce black velvet. It was hardly a cockney's drink, but they appeared to like it, particularly once we had made our way northwards across the Seine into areas of greater female habitation.

At B7 wasps were a bigger pest than visitors. They were dangerous too. They swarmed over everything sweet and you had to keep your eyes open no matter what you were eating. A wasp nearly cost us a pilot. He was drinking a mug of tea one afternoon, and like most pilots was talking at the same time. The wasp slipped unnoticed into his mug and when he swallowed it stung him in the throat. The boy's throat rapidly closed up and he began to suffocate. Fortunately, one of our doctors was handy and forced a tube down his throat to keep it open, or he could well have died.

No praise would be too high for the five doctors who served in 123 Wing. They and their orderlies did a wonderful job, dealing with the many medical problems of a large, four-squadron mobile wing. Like the Good Shepherd, they even went further and rounded up many of the stray 'sheep' that are always the innocent victims of every battlefield. Squadron Leader Gryspeerdt wrote in his report to me:

> During July and August, we held a 'civil clinic' every morning at the village school at Vaussieux, a village near the Caen-Bayeux road. This was primarily intended for continuation of treatment of refugee civilian casualties from Caen and the surrounding districts, as there were no French civil doctors in our area. The Clinic became a small centre for medical as well as minor surgical treatment as soon as the word was passed around the local villages, but at no time were the attendances excessive in numbers—15 to 20 cases a day was the average, with an additional few bedridden cases unable to visit the clinic—so that this extra work never interfered with the normal running of the sick quarters. When we left Vaussieux on 1 September, the clinic treatment and case book was sealed and handed to the local Mayor, who was arranging for treatments to be carried on at Bayeux.

A number of babies were delivered at this 'civil clinic' and operations were also performed. One of our doctors operated on a Caen doctor's daughter and saved her life by extracting a shell splinter from her brain. Our gallant doctors were men of great dedication and expertise and the wing could never have functioned without them.

I was leaning on my crutches one afternoon, talking to Trafford Leigh-Mallory who had just arrived on the strip, when a Typhoon came in fast with its wheels up. It landed on the clay emergency strip alongside our metal-meshed runway and finished up in a great ball of dust almost directly in front of us. As we walked over to it and the atmosphere cleared, out stepped Paul Ezanno, CO of 198 Squadron. He sprang to attention, saluted, bowed and began to apologize as only the French know how.

Why he had not baled out I'll never know—his aircraft was shot to pieces. He was a tremendous low-attack pilot and as brave as a lion, but he had been shot down twice before within the previous few days. I told him he was finished with operational flying until further notice, yet that evening he came to see me. He was heartbroken. He told me that driving the Boche from France was his obsession and it outweighed all other considerations, even death. Although he pleaded with me, I did not give him the chance to be shot down again, not while he served with 123 Wing.

Another morning I was out among the Typhoons on the marshalling area watching the ground staff stripped to the waist and hard at work. I was wearing a plain khaki shirt, with no hat or badges of rank. A Spitfire pulled in and a smartly dressed wing commander lowered himself to the ground. He spoke rather harshly to some of my fitters and demanded to have his aircraft refuelled. I was about to blast his head off when he came over to my jeep and told me to drive him to the commanding officer. That suited me fine.

After a silent drive to our orchard headquarters site, I dropped him off at the operations caravan and said I would tell the adjutant to advise the commanding officer of his presence. I did not change my dress but just sat down at my desk, finished a cigarette, then phoned the adjutant to show the visitor in.

As the gentleman from the Air Ministry entered, he immediately realized his *faux pas* and his complexion turned fiery red. He began stammering incoherently and looked as if he wanted to sit down. He did not get the chance. Ours was a brief encounter and a lonely Spitfire was soon winging its way back to England. I later regretted the haste with which I had acted, but my ground staff meant more to me than an uninvited visitor from across the Channel, Air Ministry included. Many years later he was knighted for his service in the postwar Air Force, so perhaps our short sharp meeting taught him to be more tolerant than the young New Zealand group captain who commanded 123 Wing at the time of his visit.

Once the Germans were either killed, captured or driven out of Normandy, the advance towards the Rhine began in earnest. We moved the wing three times in little more than a week. Our first move was to B23, in a rather pleasant area near Morainville. However, we spent only two days there, and since I was already planning to cross the Seine to B35 near Le Tréport, I saw little of Morainville, or its brand new airstrip. B35 was a plain clay strip and I was constantly worried in case it rained. One good downpour would have bogged us down for the duration.

It was from Le Tréport that I flew across to Newchurch in the Romney Marshes to attend my long-delayed Tangmere farewell party. 486 was based there, flying Tempests in pursuit of flying bombs. Before leaving to cross the Channel, my fitter and rigger filled the gun bays of my Typhoon with about four dozen bottles of champagne. Then I took off and climbed over a high belt of cloud which covered the Channel. Letting down before coming into land I noticed what I thought were thin streams of petrol leaving the trailing edge of both wings. It had me puzzled, but on landing the mystery was soon solved. The altitude and the vibration had been too much for some of the cargo in the gun bays and the bottles had blown their corks.

It proved a happy, if heavy, evening and I was eventually put to bed on the high narrow operating table in station sick quarters. Not that I needed medical attention; they were simply short of what they considered suitable beds for a senior officer. In my condition, I could have slept on my head in a chicken coop.

The next morning I had a rude awakening. Someone blew up a flying bomb almost directly over the airfield and a shower of plaster fell from the ceiling. I learnt afterward that it was Jim McCaw—the boy who had been so fond of Tangmere meat pies. He had finished his rest period and was back with his old squadron.

I could not face breakfast and flew back to Le Tréport in time for our 9 o'clock conference. My head was heavy, but the doctors compensated for this by cutting off my plaster. The leg emerged looking like a starved rake handle and almost as useless. However, it was good to be free of my heavy appendage and within a few days I could walk quite well without a stick.

Our next move was to St Omer in the Pas de Calais, directly inland from Cap Griz Nez. The reconnaissance party proceeded by road while I flew ahead in the Auster, taking my fitter, Corporal Franks, along for the ride. St Omer did not impress me. Although it was a permanent aerodrome previously used by the Luftwaffe, I considered its runways were too short for our Typhoons, and I was about to fly to Group HQ at Londinières, inland from Dieppe, when an English-speaking Frenchman informed me that the Germans had just vacated Merville, a large permanent airfield near Lille.

We flew low and cautiously approached Merville from the west before landing on its perimeter track because delayed-action bombs were spread out intermittently over both runways. This did not worry the French and we were soon surrounded by a cheering multitude. I made up my mind that Merville not St Omer, was to be our next move. But we had no wireless in our Auster and my decision meant flying back to Group HQ and also informing the reconnaissance party of the change.

By a strange coincidence a fault in our petrol gauge led to the solving of most of our problems. While flying above the main road southwest of Abbeville, we noticed the gauge was stationary in the nearly empty position. There were no suitable fields below us and the only thing we could do was land on the road, but convoys were streaming north and it was difficult to find a gap. After buzzing a line of vehicles, a space opened up and we were able to put ourselves down in one piece. Amazingly, the first vehicle to meet us was one of our own reconnaissance party, and behind them an army convoy loaded with rockets and petrol that belonged to one of Broadhurst's 83 Group wings. I instructed my own party to proceed to Merville and ordered the army captain to alter whatever instructions he had and offload his convoy at Merville.

Corporal Franks corrected the fault in the fuel gauge and topped us up with a jerrycan of petrol from one of our own jeeps. Two military police kept the road clear and we were soon off again and on our way to Group HQ at Londinières, where I was greeted by Air Commodore Tim McEvoy, our SASO, and promptly asked what I thought of St Omer. I said I did not, and that we were going to Merville. Tim was rather surprised that the Germans had left it, but informed me that we could not go there anyway as no provision had been made to stock it with rockets and petrol.

Although I felt rather guilty at diverting one of Broadhurst's convoys, I had to tell him that he need not worry, as provisions had already been taken care of. The RAF Regiment bomb disposal experts had the Merville runways clear in a matter of hours and we flew in the squadrons the next day. In terms of self-reliance it was the best move we ever made.

During our various moves from one airfield to another the squadrons were never idle. Le Havre, Boulogne, Calais and Dunkirk were still garrisoned by Hitler's armies, and by-passed by our main forces. With Group HQ also trying to keep up with the rapid advance towards the Rhine, communications with our wing would often be disrupted and we became like the early Crusaders, conducting our own private war. If our army liaison officers requested our presence away back at Le Havre, we gladly obliged, and we were as ready to fly to Calais, Dunkirk or Boulogne. In fact, if necessary, we could have our squadrons operating over all four places at once. However, most of our effort went into belting the enemy forces rapidly gathering in the Breskens pocket, an area just north-east of Bruges opposite the Walcheren Island port of Flushing.

Summer was now on the wane, and although the long-drawn-out battle for Normandy was behind us, whenever my thoughts drifted back across the Seine it was always with a depth of feeling and a sense of loss for all those boys of our wing who had fallen. The sounds of youth still echoed from the mess bar, but now many of our pilots were comparative strangers. The older hands who had weathered the flak storms were much quieter. Their faces were like pages from a well worn book, reflecting the agonies of the past and the dismal warnings for the future. There was to be no respite. They knew, as I did, that the nearer we approached the tiger's cage, the more lethal became its teeth and claws.

11
Walcheren

Merville airfield was one hell of a place. Its long concrete runways were a luxury for our Typhoons. But the mud that was everywhere else, and the flat uninteresting country that surrounded us, were most depressing. Soon after we arrived a pilot undershot the runway, overturned in soft ground, and was drowned in the mud before we could extricate him.

We nearly lost 609 Squadron's goat, too. Billy, a large, short-haired, long-horned animal, had been with the squadron since the early days of the war. He accompanied it to Normandy, and few of the pilots would take to the air without first going through the ritual of saluting him. He would eat almost anything, being particularly partial to cigarettes and starter cartridges, spitting the brass caps out of the side of his mouth like corks from a pop gun.

When we arrived at Merville, he was tethered near a large heap of ersatz stuffing that had once filled an old mattress from a nearby barrack block. It looked like wood shavings and was meant for him to sleep on, but he made a hefty meal of it during the night. In the morning most of it was gone and he was blown out like a barrage balloon, cross-eyed and bleating for attention. I do not know what Flying Officer Bell his squadron doctor did for him, but he survived. A few days later I caught him on the bonnet of my station wagon, busily making a meal of the windscreen wipers.

I led my first operational show from Merville against a German headquarters on the outskirts of Le Havre. We swept in low on a large cream-coloured concrete building and our rockets reduced it to rubble, sending up showers of concrete and other debris. We met little flak, but I felt as if someone was boring into my left cheekbone with

136

a chisel, and my mind flashed back to the Dutch collaborators we had taken aboard ship at Curaçao.

Bomber Command dropped a further 5,000 tons of bombs on Le Havre in a single daylight raid, and the 11,000-strong garrison surrendered on 11 September. Twelve months previously to the day I had hammered into an E-boat as it was about to pass through the moles at Le Havre. A lot had happened since my last birthday.

To brighten up our lives in our dreary new surroundings I ordered our first mixed party since arriving on the Continent. I left it to the Belgian boys to find the girls, and they did an excellent job. Beautiful young women arrived—as did the champagne—in three-ton trucks, and our catering staff put on a banquet fit for royalty. It was a huge success, although it was some days before we managed to get rid of the last of our visitors. They kept popping out from all sorts of places.

A few days later Group Captain 'Johnnie' Walker arrived at Merville with his 135 Wing and established himself on the south side of the aerodrome. 135 was a Spitfire wing and included 485 (New Zealand) Squadron. Johnnie, a dark and handsome Englishman, was one of the nicest RAF types I ever met, cast in the same pleasant mould as Paddy Crisham, 'Dizzy' Allen and that master of English amateur golf, Wing Commander 'Laddie' Lucas. Like all true gentlemen they were extremely polite and made me feel like a young barnyard cousin.

Within a short time of their arrival 135 Wing put on a party, too. I accepted an invitation, but told Johnnie that I might be a bit late as I was already committed to a cocktail evening in Béthune on the same night. That day a new padre was posted to 123 Wing—a short, thick-set Welshman who, I learned later, had been an outstanding rugby fly-half. I took him with me to Béthune, and when we came back to Merville and joined Johnnie's party at about 10 pm it was in full swing. We arrived in the middle of a conga and the long snakelike procession was winding its way around the dance hall, to the steady jungle beat of the band's tom-toms. There would have been nothing unusual in this, but most of the women were naked, except for their high heeled shoes.

Taking the padre by the arm, I remarked that indulging in such behaviour was hardly in keeping with the cloth, but he made it clear that there was nothing shameful in the female form and was determined to join in. By this time his eyes were sparkling and sticking out like a bullfrog's, and before I could add to my protestations he was sandwiched between two tall blondes, flicking his hips out, first to the left and then to the right, in time with the best of them. It was a sight I find hard to describe, and needless to say he became the most popular padre we ever had.

By the time we arrived at Merville, not far from the Belgian border, two of our squadrons were commanded by stout-hearted Belgians. Monty van Lierde, DFC, had 164, and 'Cheval' Lallemant, DFC, was leading 609. All four squadrons were a potpourri of many nations—khaki-clad South Africans; New Zealanders, including two Maori boys, Milich and Kirch; Canadians; Australians; and an Argentinian, Pancho Pagnam, who might have been a younger version of film star James Cagney. If Pancho had been knocked down seven days a week he would still have risen from the floor, swinging both fists.

There was also Klaus Hugo Adam, a German-born Jew who later made a name for himself as art director of the James Bond films. Quiet and polite, he was an excellent low-attack pilot. Only he knew what lay ahead of him, had he been shot down and captured by the Nazis. While in Normandy I had recommended him for a commission, but the Air Ministry turned it down. I considered that if he was willing to offer his life for 123 Wing, he was worthy of holding the King's Commission, and I dropped an informal note to this effect to the foreign Secretary, my friend of the tennis court, Mr Anthony Eden. However, 'Heinie' Adam was not to receive his commission until December 1944, through the usual channels of 84 Group HQ.

I was proud to be their commander, but I was always aware that no one man makes a successful wing. A wing, like any enterprise, had to have a boss, and I just happened to be there at the right time. Every department, every individual, was a vital part of our large team, and we carried out our duties to the best of our ability—no matter what rank or station. It was satisfying, frequently exhilarating, and very often sad.

After weathering the triumphs and tragedies of Normandy and the blistering heat of battle, Dring had become my brother. We had always got on well, even away back in our Tangmere days, but now we were veterans, drawn closer by the forces of survival. The day Le Havre fell I had reached my 26th birthday; Dring was little older. We had, in the previous four years, lived through a thousand lifetimes. We had become products of the battle skies, and of the cold, hard facts of war. During the day we did not see much of each other, for unlike Spitfire squadrons, Typhoons normally ferreted around the battle zone in small formations, and it was a full-time job for him conducting the many briefings that were part of our close-support operations. In front of the squadron personnel I was always 'Sir' and he 'Dring', but in the evenings, when flying was finished, we would meet in my caravan and discuss the day's activities, and on the same level. Then he became 'Dringo' and I 'Scottie'. A drink or two, and he always seemed to finish back on his Lincolnshire farm.

I too had spent most of my childhood surrounded by sheep and horses, and we talked about farming well into the night. It diverted our minds from the menacing skies, the mud of Merville and the thousand fears of an unknown future. While 'Dringo' drifted across the green pastures of his native England, my own mind was 12,000 miles away on the other side of the world, floating back to the tussocks of the high country, the warm, brown scented hills dotted with wild briar and grazing sheep. I heard again the music of the clear mountain streams where I used to fish, the haunting call of wild geese as they skeined high in the evening sky.

On 14 September the ever-smiling 'Cheval' Lallemant was hit by flak. His aircraft caught fire, but he was unable to bale out because shrapnel had damaged his canopy release mechanism. However, he force-landed at base and fought his way out of the blazing wreckage, badly burning his hands in the process. 'Cheval' had commanded his squadron for a month, which was much longer than some. Ian Waddy had joined me in Normandy to command 164 Squadron, but was shot down before he even had a chance to have a good look around. 'Cheval' was patched up in England and he later returned to flying, but Ian became a guest of the German government and finished the war as a POW.

It was at Merville that I said my last farewell to Trafford Leigh-Mallory. It was there, too, that I acted as arbitrator between Bill Jordan and a short, bald-headed, elderly New Zealand group captain by the name of 'Tiny' White. Our High Commissioner had decided to come over to France for the day. As he boarded his aircraft at Heston, White, who was visiting Britain, asked if he could tag along too. Mr Jordan agreed, and once airborne he asked the group captain about his companion. 'Tiny' had had the audacity to invite his own photographer along. Bill reacted like a bull to a red rag. If a photographer were required he could well provide one himself. To Jordan, who had weathered the London blitz, all New Zealand non-combatant wartime visitors were 'Lambton Quay Squatters', Lambton Quay being the Wellington street where the seat of New Zealand's government was situated.

So it was a disgruntled-looking trio that left the aircraft on arrival at Merville. At the start of the war I had met the group captain while I was a 'sprog' trainee at Levin. He had once stopped me and ordered me to have my hair cut. It had been cut the day before, and I had politely said so, but he told me to have it cut again—and like his. He had lifted his cap to illustrate his requirements; he was as bald as a tin plate. I had not forgotten this encounter and packed him off to Johnnie Walker's wing with one of my junior pilots as his guide.

The High Commissioner seemed to enjoy his day and he was even polite to White as they boarded the plane for their return to England. I gave his aircraft an escort of six Typhoons as far as Cap Griz Nez, and I heard later that this attention had pleased him immensely. As far as our New Zealand operational pilots were concerned, Bill Jordan was the most popular man in the United Kingdom.

On 17 September, Montgomery's Arnhem operation, called Market Garden, got off to a bad start. Ill-conceived and doomed to fail before it began, it was an operation that depended almost entirely on the weather. Had 2nd TAF had more to say in its execution, there was a good chance that Market Garden would have taken on a different shape, but its success would still have been doubtful. The planning and control of these airborne landings was not carried out by the commanders on the spot, but was handled by a combined headquarters in England, which was like trying to conduct an orchestra from across the Channel.

More than 1,000 bombers paved the way to the dropping zones, and 1,200 fighters supported the airborne landings. Altogether 4,600 aircraft were employed on the first day, and only 73 were shot down, almost all by flak. This original number did not include aircraft of the 2nd TAF, which flew nearly 600 sorties in support of Lieutenant-General Brian Horrocks and his 30 Corps, who were to push their way northwards and link up with the airborne forces.

2nd TAF was kept out of the actual dropping zone because the planners feared we might clash with the American fighters! We felt sorry for all those brave army troops fighting a desperate battle against great odds north of Eindhoven. My sympathies lay with 30

Corps, too. Its pathway across the sodden country would hardly support a human foot, let alone the tanks and other vehicles of modern war. To the pilots, Market Garden was an immense blunder. But we were only the implements, the tools of the trade, and had no say in policy.

We continued our efforts to clear the Germans from the Channel ports. They fought ferociously, with a fanaticism born of desperation. The tide of war, which had taken the Americans up to and over the German frontier and the British and Canadians into Belgium and Holland, had rushed past the Pas de Calais, leaving there a large hotchpotch of disorganized enemy formations drifting into the strongly garrisoned Channel ports. When the Hitler order came for them to hold on at all costs, there began that elimination of awkward 'pockets' and coastal garrisons which was destined to be a prior commitment of Canadian Army/84 Group for some time.

These were no mere 'mopping up' operations. The Breskens Pocket and Walcheren Island, for example, which were still ahead of us, were major operations of vital importance. And that we had to look forwards as well as backwards meant that at one time 600 of our own troops were 'besieging' up to 14,000 enemy troops in Dunkirk. By flooding the country round Dunkirk, the Germans had literally sealed themselves in, and although without air support their chances of escape were virtually nil, they fought with everything they possessed.

While we advanced from the Seine to the Rhine, within the space of a month, Bomber Command dropped 25,000 tons of bombs on these besieged ports. At Boulogne a single raid by 762 bombers was unable to neutralize the defenders completely, some positions on the high coastal strip to the south of the port holding out after the main attack had succeeded. When they were called on to surrender under the threat of further bombing, no reply was received and two squadrons of our Typhoons were sent over the target area. As they circled preparatory to attacking, up went the white flag and the aircraft were called off.

Boulogne fell on 22 September, eleven days after Le Havre. Calais surrendered on 1 October after a series of attacks in which 1,637 bombers dropped 8,000 tons in five days. Whether this heavy bombing was justified or not did not concern me at the time, but I had to agree with my old chief, Leigh-Mallory, who later declared:

I feel that in the broad view, this bombing effort would have been more profitably directed against targets inside Germany, particularly as the disorganization of the retreating army was most acute at this time. I should have been happier to see it used against focal points in the communication system behind the enemy frontier, in an effort to delay the movement of reinforcements with which the enemy succeeded, in mid-September, in stabilizing a line along the Rhine and Moselle.

I also felt that Montgomery had grown too dependent on Bomber Command, so that its efforts were often directed away from their proper role of stabbing deep at the source of Germany's war production.

Wing Commander Johnnie Checketts, a New Zealand Spitfire ace who led a wing at Biggin Hill, was staying with me the day Calais fell, and we motored into the battered city hot on the heels of the army, more out of curiosity than in the course of duty. It was a staggering sight, and also a very productive expedition. We came upon a German underground bunker full of frozen pork, blocks of apple sauce, frozen green peas and case upon case of Portuguese sardines. Small mobs of young pigs were running loose amongst the bomb-shattered buildings. We caught one of these little porkers, put him in a box, and filled the rest of the station wagon with cases of sardines.

When we left for Merville one of our back tyres could not stand the strain and blew out with a loud explosion. Darkness was approaching and we had some difficulty in changing the wheel. Also, before we had finished, a lone sniper began his own private war. Bullets began whining close and although I did not think they were aimed directly at us, as soon as the spare wheel was fitted we made a hurried exit—still with our little porker but minus a few cases of sardines. When we arrived back in Merville I instructed my transport and catering officers to send a convoy into Calais to take care of the delicacies we had left behind. For the first week in October we dined exceedingly well.

That night Johnnie, Dring and I went into Lille and met up with Wing Commander Alan Deere, who was on the staff at 84 Group Control Centre. We went to a night club and drank more than was good for us. The floor show was similar to one I had witnessed in Panama City on my way to England: all flesh and feathers. Dring summed it up dryly in his own quiet way: 'Wish the band would play up a bit. I can't hear the music for fly buttons hitting the roof.'

Next day we had enormous hangovers, but the war had to go on. I had previously notified Group HQ that I would fly an Auster up into Belgium and reconnoitre my next airfield, at Ursel, near the village of Eeklo halfway between Ghent and Bruges. It had been used by the Italians during the Battle of Britain and there was some doubt as to the suitability of its runway.

It was a beautiful afternoon and I invited Johnnie Checketts along. We flew low and with our side windows down—more to cool our heads than as a visual aid. The ground below and ahead was still under German occupation and long before we reached Ursel tracer appeared directly ahead of us. Since Austers were not made to do battle, we were forced to beat a hasty retreat.

Once back over friendly territory near Lille, Johnnie began visibly showing signs of the effects of the night before. He hung his head out of the window into the slipstream and appeared to be asleep. I could not resist the temptation to pull my 38 calibre Smith and Wesson from its holster, put my arm out past his head, and pull the trigger. He shot bolt upright, his bloodshot eyes like pink saucers. Johnnie was six years my senior, but being very much a boy at heart we were soon rocking the little plane with our laughter.

Our operational missions were still wide and varied. We were employed mostly under VCP control and often worked on targets within yards of our own troops. The standard of close support became as near perfect as it could ever be. We had Canadian and British army officers attached to our wing as interested observers and it seemed a pity to me that my own country's army was missing out on this golden opportunity. So on a flying visit to London I went to Halifax House and told Brigadier R. S. Park, the head of our army mission, that I would welcome the presence on my wing of some of our New Zealand regular army officers. He seemed vaguely interested and promised to pass on my request to Wellington. However, I heard no more on the matter, and thus the New Zealand army lost the opportunity to observe at first hand our air-to-ground close-support techniques.

Our rockets could out-gun the dreaded German 88s and explode her heaviest tanks; yet the New Zealand army was still playing around with its 25-pounders. That gun was eventually retired from service on 12 September 1977—some 33 years later!

*

Although the campaign in Europe was almost halfway through and we were rapidly approaching the Rhine, the Air Ministry had still not decided what constituted a tour for our low-attack Typhoon pilots. In Bomber Command it was 30 trips. A total of 200 operational flying hours made up the tour of a Spitfire pilot, although this was left to the discretion of the pilot's commanding officer, for a home-based Spitfire pilot in the North of England could complete a recognized tour without firing his guns.

The chances of a Bomber Command pilot surviving a tour were already well known, but for the low-attack Typhoon pilot, in terms of flying hours, the chances of survival were even less. The Air Ministry treated us like fighter pilots, yet in Normandy, for instance, many of our trips lasted only ten to fifteen minutes, and each time our aircraft were at the mercy of the light flak. When hit, the pilot was normally too low to bale out. Unhappily the squadron commanders ran the same risks as the new pilots, and some hardly lasted long enough even to learn the names of their own pilots. It was not until December, when we were in Holland, that the qualifications for a tour were settled as 80 sorties, though that could vary according to the types of sortie and the strain on the pilots. I would have preferred much shorter tours of, say, 40 missions followed by briefer periods of rest. But by that time the war was reaching its zenith and our supply of pilots and experienced leaders was at its lowest ebb.

We continued to hammer hard at those troops trapped in the Breskens Pocket, but bad weather restricted our activities at times, and when we were grounded some 70,000 Germans managed to escape from the pocket and make their way in barges and ferry boats to the islands of Walcheren and Beveland, and even as far as Bergen-op-Zoom. Nevertheless, we attacked many of these overcrowded vessels and inflicted heavy casualties on their occupants.

The Germans still hung grimly to the area around Breskens, and thus held both sides of the Scheldt estuary, which commanded the approach to the port of Antwerp. It was not the best of country upon which to fight offensive war and fierce and bloody fighting took place between the defenders and the Canadians. The flat landscape, particularly in the surrounding approaches, was criss-crossed by ditches and waterways, and tanks edging along the few roads were easy targets for the dug-in German forces trying to keep the Canadians at bay.

In an attempt to tip the scales in our favour, on 5 October 250 aircraft of Bomber Command, using the heaviest of bombs, breached the dyke on West Walcheren and flooded 25 square miles of the island fortress. But the heavy coastal guns, firmly bedded into the island's higher perimeter between West Kapelle and Flushing, were still high and dry and well camouflaged.

From the air this flooding looked tragic and severe. Generations of Dutchmen had struggled to win the land from the sea. I wondered at the time if, instead of flooding the island, Montgomery would have been wiser had he dropped his airborne forces on Walcheren instead of Arnhem. Antwerp was a necessary stepping-stone to cross the Rhine and we needed it badly, but Walcheren, even though largely flooded, still held the key to the Scheldt.

Although the hot breath of battle could always be seen rising off the combat zones, by October the cold lips of the approaching winter were already caressing the tall poplars in the Pas de Calais. Squadron Leader T. Y. 'Bob' Wallace, DFM, a tall, gangling South African, took command of 609 Squadron in place of 'Cheval' Lallemant who was in hospital; Squadron Leader A. W. Ridler replaced Paul Ezanno, DFC, in 198; the indomitable, almost indestructible, Monty van Lierde, after many close calls, was still commanding 164; and Squadron Leader R. W. Mulliner, whose soft voice and sad droopy moustache concealed a tough English interior, led 183.

On 20 October our 84 Group squadrons attacked the headquarters of the German Fifteenth Army at Dordrecht, and caused the greatest loss of life ever seen in that town. We learned soon after the attacks that more than 200 Germans had been killed, including 55 officers, 17 of senior rank—two of them generals.

The porker we had captured in Calais—christened 'Herman'—was adopted by the officers' mess, more with a view to Christmas than in sympathy for a war orphan. Herman became a great favourite with the boys, who would crowd round his makeshift sty built from old packing cases and baled straw. However, there was one member of the wing who could not stand the sight of him, and that was Billy the goat. He had obviously made up his mind that France was not big enough for both of them and we had to cover the pigsty with strong reinforced wire netting. Billy would spend hours trying to find a way into Herman's little house, and we often saw him standing at full stretch on his hind legs, looking down into the pig's straw-floored bunker. You could read the message in his eyes.

Ursel was eventually cleared of the enemy and I flew up and landed an Auster on the single concrete runway. It was 600 yds too short for our requirements, so I notified the airfield construction engineers. As always, they rapidly complied, but they soon ran into a major problem. Between the end of the concrete and the start of the extension was a 100-yd patch of soft ground that appeared to have no bottom. They bulldozed it out and filled it with clinker and bomb rubble, then levelled out the whole extension and overlaid it with bitumenized hessian, laid by a machine that reeled it on to the smooth hard earth surface in continuous long wide strips and cemented the widths together. So long as the undersurface was free of too much moisture, this type of runway was satisfactory for a limited period, and it was certainly much better than a bare, dry surface easily affected by weather.

As on wire mesh runways, no crash-landings were permitted, for a wheels-up landing would tear the surface to pieces and make it unoperational. Anyone forced to crash-land had to take his chance on the bomb-scarred areas beside the runway.

We shifted from Merville to Ursel on 29 October and for the first day or two the new airstrip stood up well. But we soon found ourselves in trouble. There must have been a spring under the filled area, for moisture seeped under the artificial surface, and when an aircraft was landing the vacuum created in its wake lifted the hessian from the runway. The hessian would then rise to a height of six or eight feet and follow the aircraft in a smooth grey wave for 50 or 60 yards before falling into place again. This did not happen with aircraft taking off as the blast from their propellers would flatten anything. Even on landing the leading aircarft was quite safe, as the wave was behind it. But pilots landing behind another aircraft had to make sure they stayed well back, or their aircraft props could be ploughing in to the airborne runway. Had the large prop of a Typhoon collected a wave it would not only have destroyed our airstrip but capsized the offending aircraft and created havoc amongst those immediately following.

I did not like the place, but it was from this airfield that 123 Wing saved Montgomery from yet another disaster, so when we left a few days later, I looked at Ursel with a certain measure of gratitude and affection.

Breskens had fallen on 22 October, but the Germans were still holding Walcheren, thus denying us the waterway to Antwerp which our armies had captured as early as 4 September. By this time the need for Antwerp as a port was becoming acute and materials required for the advance were being rationed to a degree which interfered with military efficiency.

So the planning staff decided on an all-out assault on the island of Walcheren on 1 November. This was to take the form of a two-pronged attack—one directed on Flushing and the other through the breached dyke at West Kapelle, where Royal Navy craft hoped to sail straight in. As is often the case at this time of year, the weather over the Low Countries had been unfavourable, and the softening-up operations against the island were severely curtailed. Nor were prospects for the day of the assault any better. But the urgency of opening up the Scheldt outweighed this consideration and the attack could not be postponed.

The morning of 1 November was one I shall never forget. A cold black drizzle hid the far side of our aerodrome. The cloud ceiling seemed to weigh heavy on my shoulders, and flying appeared out of the question. I had hardly finished my early morning cup of tea when group operations were on the phone. By the sound of despair and resignation in my caller's voice I knew immediately that the seaborne assault forces were in deep trouble.

The control vessel, HMS *Warspite*, and her two attendant monitors, stationed off West Kapelle to cover the landings, were in the temporary category of obsolescent. Their spotter planes had been grounded in England by fog and, to add to this, all 2nd TAF airfields were fogbound. Allied commandos had gained a toehold on Flushing under cover of darkness, but 25 landing craft approaching the island's south coast were being picked off like flies by heavy German batteries built into the higher ground between West Kapelle and Flushing. Nine craft had been sunk and eleven others put out of action.

I left my caravan and walked out on to the airstrip. The ground was lower there and visibility improved a little. I knew Dring could read my thoughts, but I did not discuss the pros and cons: the responsibility of taking my squadrons into the air or keeping them on the ground was mine alone. Bad weather can wipe out a wing faster than flak, but the flight path to the troubled area was as flat as a seascape, and so I decided we must take the risk.

Every pilot on this early-morning mission knew of the dangers, and the briefing tent was quieter than usual. I would lead, and as an emergency measure the wing would operate as two formations. The first two squadrons would follow me, and, unless I changed my mind in the air, Dring would take off with the other two.

There was no wind and we could take off almost directly into our line of flight. We were soon skimming over the flat land on our run out to the coast near the waterlogged area surrounding Breskens. Within two or three minutes my prayers were answered. The cloud base began to lift to about 500 ft and the forward visibility improved considerably. The sea was like glass and in a short time we were on patrol off the island's coast between West Kapelle and Flushing.

Below was the devastatingly tragic sight of total war. Soldiers were struggling among the debris that floated on patches of blood-stained sea. Others seemed to be just lying on the water. Some waved. I could see no rescue boats in the vicinity. To make matters worse it was a moment or two before the well-camouflaged heavy coastal batteries barked out their messages of death and we could pinpoint the seat of the trouble. But immediately we saw their flashes we answered them back and every time a gun fired, four Typhoons set upon it. As though stirred by the scene below, each pilot pressed home his attack almost into the gun barrels. Rockets exploded against the steel and concrete, sometimes in pairs, sometimes in salvoes. Flak flew in all directions, but we raked the flak guns with our cannon fire. We kept the pressure on, and before long the guns along the southern perimeter of the island ceased to fire.

While we attacked the guns, commandos of the 4th Special Service Brigade took advantage of the diversion and landed almost unscathed on either side of the gap that had been opened by Bomber Command on 3 October. Some sailed straight through the breach and attacked West Kapelle from the east.

Luckily the weather had improved over our Ursel airstrip and we had no difficulty in regaining our base. As the weather improved the wing carried out many more attacks on other parts of the island's defences throughout the day. We felt our mission had been well accomplished, and to confirm our view, that evening we received a signal from Admiral Ramsay, the Allied Naval Commander-in-Chief, Europe:

The timely and well executed support by your Rocket Firing Typhoons when 80% of the landing craft were out of action, undoubtedly was a vital factor in turning the scales to our advantage.

Many of us had sore heads next morning, and it was not because they had grown too big for our shoulders. We learned later that a number of our rockets had actually found their way through the apertures and past the guns and had burst against the concrete walls inside. The concussion had plastered the interior walls and ceilings with flesh and blood. It was interesting, but news I could well have done without.

By 3 November the first minesweeper flotilla sailed up the Scheldt as far as Terneuzen and began clearing a 70-mile channel from the North Sea to Antwerp, which took 100 minesweepers three weeks to achieve. The first Allied convoy triumphantly entered Antwerp on 28 November.

Although we rocketed our way forward towards Germany we still had to look over our shoulder at Dunkirk. It seemed a waste of time and aircraft, but we were told the port was part of the overall plan, and we acted on instructions. Many miles behind the battlefront, and besieged by the Czech Brigade, the Germans in Dunkirk still fought like wounded tigers, and in the process claimed another of my squadron commanders. While attacking the main German ration store in the centre of the town, Bob Wallace of 609 was hit by flak and crashed in flames. Like his predecessor, 'Cheval' Lallemant, he had commanded his squadron for barely a month.

We promoted a flight commander from 164 Squadron to take his place. Charles de Moulin, DFC, was a blond, crinkly-haired Belgian who for some reason or other was given the nickname 'Windmill Charlie'. He was one of the happiest and friendliest pilots on the wing. Like 'Spud' Murphy in those far off Tangmere days, rank meant nothing to him, and he treated me just as he did his subordinates, always with that air of face-to-face secrecy which was born of supreme confidence.

As November drew to a close, there was still no sign of an early victory. The shorter days brought no respite. While the Canadians struggled eastwards in line with the Maas, they were continually calling for our assistance, and we carried out many low-attack operations under VCP control.

With their backs to the Rhine, the German armies were protecting their last line of defence on the Western Front. If that was lost, so was their war. All the signs pointed to one conclusion: the Germans would rather die fighting for the Fatherland than suffer the indignity of being forced back and drowned in Hitler's last ditch.

12

Ardennes—the Last Offensive

On 26 November we moved out of Ursel to our next base at Gilze Rijen in Holland. It was only 12 miles from the battle line, and like Merville had two long permanent runways. But instead of surrounding mud, there were plenty of aircraft bays, most of them hidden among small pine trees. These not only sheltered our ground staff from the icy winds, but also provided some welcome natural camouflage.

The airfield's domestic complex lay some miles away from the aerodrome and consisted of beautiful brick buildings, constructed for our Luftwaffe opponents in a style reminiscent of our most modern RAF stations. Surrounded by pine forest, each building was centrally heated. It was a far cry from our tents and caravans and we soon settled into the luxury of our new surroundings. Indeed our messing habits became quite formal. The wing's 14-piece orchestra would often come into the officers' mess to play during our evening meal. This excellent orchestra was made up of almost all ex-professionals, and was conducted by our Transport Officer, Flight-Lieutenant Short. It became quite famous and performed a Christmas broadcast for the BBC.

I kept my caravan on the airfield, but December was far too cold to have my pilots sitting around in canvas dispersal tents, so I instructed the local burgomaster to organize a workforce and build a large, barn-like brick building among the pine trees near my caravan. It was the first time I had seen this industrious nation at work. They had the building completed in less than five days and the pilots were soon sitting round an enormous fireplace which we fed with pine logs the size of railway sleepers. Tedder visited us the day we opened this new dispersal; he looked surprised when I told him that six days earlier he would have been standing on pine needles.

On 5 December we lost yet another 609 Squadron Commander. 'Windmill Charlie' was hit by flak while attacking an oil storage depot just inside Germany. Although on fire, he managed to gain enough height to bale out and become a POW. He had been in his job for just three weeks.

Eric Roberts, DFC, who had been with us in Normandy but was forced off operations by a road accident in September, was back with the wing and was promoted to command 609. A quiet, pleasant Englishman, he was highly experienced and soon had the squadron hard at work attacking a midget-submarine base on the south side of Schouwen Island in the East Scheldt. It was a successful strike, although two of our squadrons on the same mission lost pilots, including another experienced Australian, Flight-Lieutenant Norman Merritt, DFC.

It was about this time that I was asked by the Air Ministry to attend two functions in Paris—both of which proved fairly disastrous. At the first I was to speak to the world's press; at the second I was to be guest of honour at a dinner celebrating a French Aero Club anniversary.

Appearing before a room full of war correspondents was bad enough, but one reporter among them really set me alight. She was a short, middle-aged blonde whose sagging jowls, dull eyes, and gum-chewing mouth reminded me of Herman. She kindled the flame by asking me what I thought of the Germans as a fighting race. I replied that I considered there was none better, and she blew the flames into a conflagration.

Since many Americans bore German surnames and were obviously of direct German descent, this rather surprised me. We close-support pilots could see the battle from both sides, and what I did not know from the air I learned through frequent visits to the forward combat areas. However, fighting a war was my profession—not politics— and although I stood my ground for a time, I could see there was little sense in arguing with this particular 'lady', so I cut my address short and withdrew to cooler surroundings. I am pleased to say she was typical neither of her nation nor of her calling.

The dinner was held in a large banqueting hall and all the guests were seated at the largest and most luxuriously decorated table I had ever seen. The women wore long evening gowns, the men white tie and tails, except for the few servicemen like myself who were in uniform. On either side of the table stood a long line of flunkeys. In their maroon tailcoats and black breeches and stockings they reminded me of a line-up of coloured grasshoppers.

A few days earlier 84 Group had provided me with a new interpreter. He was a young English boy, newly commissioned and straight from Oxbridge. Before leaving Gilze Rijen I had prepared what I thought was a suitable speech in reply to the Aero Club President's address of welcome. This was translated on to my interpreter's own paper, with instructions that as soon as the President had finished his speech, I would rise, bow to him and the assembled guests, and after repeating 'Vive la France' a few times, nod to my 'mouthpiece' across the table to deliver in French my carefully prepared reply.

Continental dinners can last for hours, and this feast was no exception. I should have warned my young officer across the table that the French have no time for empty glasses; as soon as a glass showed signs of depletion it was promptly topped up by one of the colourful flunkeys. Before we were halfway through dinner I noticed the boy was beginning to fumble with his silverware and his eyes looked out of focus. I reached under the table and tapped his shins, but his only response was to smile at me like the village idiot.

As the President rose to deliver his speech my interpreter slid off his chair and under the table. Two of the servants lifted him up and ceremoniously carted him out feet first, leaving me gripping the edge of the table, transfixed with fright. After the President had finished a very long speech, I rose to my feet. I managed to get in my 'Vive la France', mumbled a few words in English, and sat down again. However, the French take everything in their stride and when I said goodnight my hosts bade me farewell with the same gracious courtesy with which they had earlier received me.

At the hotel next morning I made for my interpreter's bedroom, ready to throttle him. I burst in without knocking and found him sitting up in bed with an ice-pack on his head, reading a French newspaper. Before I could open my mouth he said: 'It's all right, Sir. It's all in the paper.' Some bright reporter had picked up a copy of my speech at the dinner, and the text had been printed in full.

Air Vice-Marshal E. C. Huddleston replaced 'Bingo' Brown as our Air Officer Commanding 84 Group. Where 'Bingo' was round and jovial, Huddleston was the exact opposite. At our first meeting he gave me the impression that he was one of those over-cautious men who guard their cigarettes in musical boxes. I never got to know him well, for our paths seldom crossed, and when they did I found him rather shy and retiring. However, this lack of rapport could well have been the result of the generation gap. Whereas he was a regular officer of many years standing, I was a young war leader of a more recent generation.

Flying bombs and V2 rockets were an ever-present threat at Gilze Rijen. We were in the mouth of what was known as 'Antwerp Alley'. Flying bombs from Germany and across the river Maas would converge above our airfield on their way to Antwerp, and the sky would often snarl to the sound of their ram-jet engines. In one 24-hour period, 148 flying bombs passed over our aerodrome.

In the evening and at night their approach could be seen from a great distance. Sometimes, after the day's work was over, I would leave my caravan office, take to the skies, and try to shoot some of them down. I would fly to meet them, and as they passed under me three or four thousand feet below I would roll over, gain speed, and dive after them. They were normally too fast for a Typhoon in level flight and I had to let them get a good 200 yards ahead before opening fire, or their explosion could blow me up too. So once they overtook me, I had little time to work in. It was not polite of me to shoot them down over our own airfield, nor could I follow them far into 'Antwerp Alley', which was heavily defended by our own flak and out of bounds. My only chance was on the far side of the Maas which was in enemy territory, or in the few miles between our airfield and 'Antwerp Alley'.

I succeeded in blowing up only one in the air, but I sent several to earth where they exploded. One, unfortunately, landed close to a Dutch village, where the explosion injured several inhabitants. My only consolation was that it might otherwise have reached Antwerp and killed several hundreds. But the incident flattened my enthusiasm and henceforth I left the flying bombs to our AA gunners.

Flying bombs would often behave strangely. After lunch one day we were sitting outside the officers' mess enjoying some winter sunshine when a bomb appeared directly overhead. It circled the mess twice just above the tree tops, then made off—back towards Germany! Another time I was motoring from the airfield to the mess, accompanied by Squadron Leader Hines, my loyal senior administration officer and ever-present shadow. Suddenly we saw the bright flame of a bomb approaching on our right. Normally we took no notice of them, unless their engines stopped. When this happened they immediately keeled over, dived to the ground and exploded. This bomb passed above the station wagon at about 2,000 ft, and then its motor suddenly cut out. I slammed on the brakes and we both dived into the roadside ditch. There was dead silence. Not even a thud. It must have glided on and made a belly landing in a distant field without exploding.

In clear weather we could see the vapour trails of the V2 rockets as they streaked up from near The Hague and vanished into the stratosphere on their way to London. One rocket misbehaved and landed near a local village, smashing all the windows and stripping the paint off a large wooden building some distance away. Another day I was leading two squadrons on the look-out for rocket-launching sites, when just north of The Hague one of these monsters blasted off almost directly below. We were flying at about 6,000 ft to keep above the lighter flak and a gigantic mushroom of white smoke appeared on the ground slightly to starboard. A huge rocket sprouted from it and began swaying and staggering up towards us. As it drew nearer it quickly accelerated, flashed past, and in less than two seconds vanished into the heavens.

That same day my caravan was almost hit by a crashing Typhoon whose pilot must have been critically wounded. His aircraft came in at high speed far from the runway. It skimmed over my concrete bay and my caravan, ploughed through the pine forest beyond, scything down trees like matchsticks, and finally came to rest in a jagged heap of twisted, steaming metal, its Napier Sabre engine some distance further on. Strangely, it did not catch fire.

To ease the burden on Antwerp we carried out many attacks against flying bomb storage depots and transport services across the river Maas. These attacks not only helped prevent the supply of flying bombs to the Germans but also assisted the Canadian Army. For instance, in December the destruction of the Vianen bridge considerably hampered enemy movement when they were gathering their forces for a further assault.

In mid-December we had another visit from General Eisenhower, and he impressed me even more than during his visit to Thorney Island. After addressing all the pilots, he took me aside and, dropping all formality, he called me 'Skarty' and thanked me at some length for the assistance 123 Wing had given his armies in their march towards the Rhine. It was a simple, sincere message that only a man of his stature would think about, compose and deliver. He was the only man for the job—a true gentleman, a great diplomat and a brilliant co-ordinator.

Later that month the prospect of victory by Christmas that Montgomery had predicted vanished in the large black cloud that suddenly appeared over the Ardennes. We had received startling news from our agents across the Maas, confirmed by our own photographic reconnaissance, that the Germans were massing for an offensive against the flank of First Canadian Army with the aim of pushing through to Antwerp. We doubled the guards on our aircraft and airfield and introduced the tightest security measures.

Then Field-Marshal von Rundstedt launched a massive counter-attack designed to split the American forces and cut off the British and Canadian armies in a sweep towards Antwerp. It was an ambitious operation, a last desperate plunge. And it could not have come at a worse time for the Allied air forces. It was mid-winter. The days were at their shortest, and already on some days flying was impossible.

After the long drag up from the dust of Normandy and the mud of the Low Countries, the personnel of my wing were nicely settled in the comfort of permanent buildings, and I had hoped they would be rewarded for their efforts by remaining at Gilze Rijen until the spring. But it was not to be. I was invited to dine with my new AOC at group HQ in Tilburg, and there he informed me that General Montgomery required my wing's presence in the Ardennes. I must, therefore, move it to A87, away to the south of Chièvres.

I knew the country well from the air. Its poor winter weather was not the least of its undesirable characteristics for close support work. I felt we could cover the Ardennes far better from our present base at Gilze. Admittedly, it meant sacrificing two rockets per aircraft in place of an extra fuel tank, but we would be working from a much more stable foundation to combat the weather problem. But no arguing wound convince my AOC. If Montgomery needed us in the Ardennes, then in God's name we must go. It was hard to believe. The very General we had slogged our guts out for was now calling the tune. He had never once visited my wing, yet he was dictating a move that should have been the prerogative of our own service.

Snow was already falling in southern Belgium, and as I drove back to Gilze Rijen I had a strong premonition that by leading my wing into the Ardennes I was moving it towards disaster.

Next day I set off with 'Hinie' to reconnoitre our new base at A87. I intended to fly down, but the weather put this out of the question, so we set off by jeep on the long journey south. We took turns at the wheel. Sleet was falling, the roads were icy, and to add to the danger we kept running into masses of supercooled fog. As soon as this fog hit anything solid it turned to 'Rhine ice', with which no windscreen wiper can cope. The glass became an ice shield and in order to stay on the road and keep going we drove with our heads out of the side of the jeep. Several times we slid off the road and had to be dragged back on, sometimes by truck, once by a Sherman tank.

That night we stayed in a private home in a small village to the south of Aalst. It was rather embarrassing to knock at the door of a strange house and demand beds for the night, but we were accepted, though somewhat guardedly. With the Germans on the move, it was no doubt difficult for the owners to decide which side to favour. One day they could be surrounded by Americans, and the next by returning Germans. Our beds were as cold as the frozen countryside, but we were given two fried eggs for breakfast, and a warm if anxious farewell.

We arrived at A87 at about 10 am and found the airfield smothered in American Thunderbolts. Since we were now in the American sector, this was not altogether surprising, but according to my information these squadrons should have moved out the day before. The American commanding officer advised me that they were there to stay, and that I would have to find some other place for my wing.

We soon resolved the issue by phoning SHAEF on dual phones and asking for our respective liaison officers. My British counterpart was polite but rather unsure of the situation. Not so the American brigadier: 'Sure, Steve. Get the hell out and let the Limeys in. You should have been away yesterday.'

With our right of occupancy confirmed, the Colonel shook my hand, apologized, and said that there had obviously been some breakdown in signals. With the German armies, including many armoured divisions, pushing well into Belgium and already at Celles and Stavelot, it seemed a dangerous time for any break in communications. However, the Americans flew out the next day and as a parting gesture left us a large quantity of canned American food.

I called forward the A party and although we lost several vehicles on the way, we had settled our squadrons in by 31 December and were bracing ourselves for the storm I felt must come. Rumours flew thick and fast, but it was not the number of German divisions facing us to the east that was uppermost in my mind. It was the dreaded Colonel Count Otto Skorzeny.

This clever, ruthless and faithful disciple of Adolf Hitler had carried out many desperate operations for his Führer, including Mussolini's rescue from captivity in 1943. He now led a Kommando brigade of American-speaking Germans, all in American uniforms and driving US tanks and jeeps. His men were to act as a 'Trojan Horse' force and seize control of the Meuse bridges between Liège and Namur. Sabotage parties in similar disguise were to infiltrate through American lines, disrupting communications and creating confusion in the rear areas.

The Germans were well aware of the striking power of our rocket Typhoons and I was fully conscious of our own vulnerability, either during darkness or if we were grounded by snow. If Skorzeny got loose among my aircraft he could 'take us to the cleaners'.

I had left 22 of our Typhoons back at Gilze, most of them under repair and maintenance or in for routine service checks. Fortunately they were well dispersed, for on the morning of 1 January the Luftwaffe staged its last major attack on the Western Front. Over 1,000 fighters, mainly FW 190s and Me 109s, threw themselves into low-level attack against 2nd Tactical Air Force airfields. Thinking we were still at Gilze, a large formation made a beeline for our dispersal areas, only to find most of our aircraft had flown. However, they managed to damage two. Some wings, particularly those in the Brussels area, fared much worse, many losing whole squadrons. A total of 155 Allied aircraft were set on fire and a further 135 badly damaged. The Luftwaffe lost 193 aircraft, many piloted by their most experienced leaders.

The visibility was too poor for enemy aircraft to attack our new base, but that night we could hear the uneven throb of the Ju 88s' engines as they groped their way in the murky darkness above.

On New Year's morning, although we had avoided the Luftwaffe's dying stabs, we were still to receive a crushing blow from the skies. It did not speed in on us with shot or shell, neither did it split open the sky with a thunderous roar. It came quietly. It stole up on us in the night, and in the morning its white mantle captured everything. We were anchored to the ground. Heavily coated, our Typhoons stood silent and dejected, their ankles deep in snow. If the enemy advanced far enough to capture the large fuel dumps the Americans had been building to the south-east of Liège, in preparation for the crossing of the Rhine, the fate of our wing would be sealed. I would have no alternative but to set fire to our Typhoons—all 60 of them—and retreat overland as best we could. It was a white nightmare and I cursed the little General for sticking his nose into what I considered was not his business.

Bulldozers and snow ploughs were soon hard at work and mountains of snow began piling up on both sides of the east-west runway. We spread truckloads of salt to help prevent freezing. But the snow kept fluttering down like big white feathers and smothered us in despair. And the news about Skorzeny's Kommandos did not help. Some 40 jeep-loads of his American-speaking troops had slipped through the crumbling US defence line and reached the Meuse. Others had cut telephone lines, intercepted despatch riders, shot up radio stations and killed military policemen. One of his audacious band had even taken over as a traffic control officer and turned an American regiment down the wrong road. We heard that Skorzeny was out to assassinate Eisenhower.

Since 123 Wing could well hold the key to the enemy's armoured success in the Ardennes, it was quite probable that we, too, were on the short list. However, as the days snowed on, the threat from the enemy armour subsided. We learned that whole Panzer divisions had run out of fuel and were bogged down just like us. But the worry was which would get mobile first, their tanks or our aircraft.

I was anxious to fly up to Gilze to see how my skeleton party had fared during the German attack on New Year's morning. However, it was not until 12 January that I could risk taking off from our runway. The snow on either side had been pushed by the bulldozers into ridges up to eight feet high and it was like flying out of a white-walled passageway. Gilze had escaped lightly and the RAF regiment attached to the station had done a tremendous job, shooting down several enemy aircraft.

After lunch I climbed into my Typhoon and rose off a nice snowless airstrip to return to the Ardennes. The weather had deteriorated and I was forced to fly just above the tree tops. To avoid having to enter cloud altogether, I veered off course to starboard, hoping to fly round a heavy black cloud. Suddenly showers of tracer came at me thick and fast. I felt several sharp thuds and pulled round hard in the direction I had come from. My diversion had taken me briefly into forbidden territory and I had entered the beehive of 'Antwerp Alley'.

Oil was streaming past the starboard window and half a cannon was missing from my port wing. Three jagged holes had been blown in the starboard outer wing, and I prayed for the sight of the Gilze runway. I was under fire for only three or four seconds, but it was long enough. The streams of red-hot tracer sent my heart racing to my throat and I cried out to God to keep my motor going. It was unbelievable. Shot down at this late hour of the war—and by our own flak!

As I hurdled an avenue of tall bare poplars, I caught sight of the Gilze runways dead ahead and reaching out towards me like open arms. I thanked God for yet another chance and made a hurried approach to the southern end of the north-south runway. I had an urgent desire to feel my feet on the ground, but I was still very conscious of the fact that a wounded Typhoon could be a dangerous companion—particularly if its legs were broken. I had seen Typhoons collapse on to the runway on their bellies and turn into screeching, uncontrollable balls of fire.

That my wheels came down and locked in the green light position was a miracle in itself, and I quickly landed my battered Typhoon with more good luck than expertise. As I left the aircraft my knees and arms were shaking and cold sweat was running down my face.

Besides lighter flak, my Typhoon had been hit three times by Bofors shells, yet it survived this pasting and carried me to safety. The motor was almost empty of oil, and a shell which had exploded in the rear fuselage had bent the armour plating and almost forced it on to the back of my head. I took another Typhoon from the servicing pool and was back in the Ardennes by mid-afternoon.

During the three weeks we were in the Ardennes we were confined to the ground for all except five days. This was most frustrating, particularly when aircraft from other wings were passing above our heads. However, they were vital days and when we shook ourselves free of the snow we wrought havoc among the German tanks and transport. Petrol wagons that were struggling forward to replenish thirsty armoured vehicles were blown to pieces, blackening the sky and surrounding snow. Tanks that were hidden under nature's white blanket were betrayed: the footprints of their crews could never be disguised. We found the tanks and turned them into funeral pyres. We had our own losses, too. One of our pilots was shot down by an American Mustang while coming in to land.

In the event, the Allied air forces had long since decided the issue in the Ardennes battle. As the Germans withdrew, or lay frozen and immobile, the value of the policies of the American Lieutenant-

General Eaker and Air Marshal Leigh-Mallory were vindicated as clearly as the blood on the Ardennes snow. No army, no matter how strong, could stay alive, let alone function, without its fuel supplies. The long arm of the strategic bomber had already played its decisive part in frustrating Hitler's last gamble.

With the battle over, we were naturally eager to return to Gilze Rijen, but the snow persisted and kept us on the ground. We were particularly irritated because our home base was working and coming over the air loud and clear, as it had done during most of our stay in the Ardennes. According to the local inhabitants it was the worst winter for 80 years. I could well believe them.

However, one morning we woke to a clear cold sky, although the horizon to the north-west was still hidden from view. Dring sent off a pilot, Flight Lieutenant Prosser, to see if the route home was safe for the four squadrons, and we listened in to his dismal tidings. He reported a huge front south of Brussels reaching out westward and to the ground, and I was forced to accept his verdict. But Dring was not convinced and asked if he could go and take a look himself. Perhaps there was a way round the bad weather. In front of his pilots I could not refuse his request, but I did not want to embarrass Prosser. Dring had been grounded for so long, I think he simply wanted to extend his wings. I said he could have a look if he so wished, but that I was quite satisfied with Prosser's report. As he took off I sat in the jeep and listened. It was the same story: we would have to wait until the weather cleared.

Dring came back over the aerodrome and started a series of aerobatic loops, rolls and stall turns. It was Dring at his best, the master of the low attack, the smiling farmer who had taken to the skies. After completing a series of slow rolls he lowered his under-carriage and began the approach. There was no wind, but he seemed to have slight starboard drift. Touching down, his aircraft ran along the runway for a few yards, swung sideways, hit the snow wall to the side of the runway, capsized and vanished in a great avalanche of snow.

For a few moments the shock paralysed me. I knew there was no hope, for the whole canopy that covered his head had been torn from the aircraft and thrown high in the air. In stunned silence we lifted his broken remains into an ambulance. I followed it towards the station sick quarters, still too shattered to accept what had happened. It was only after returning to my caravan that I felt the full impact of his death. On the chair where he sat in the evenings lay his old cherrywood pipe with its bent stem. He would suck away at it for hours and use countless matches which often burned his fingers.

Wing Commander Walter Dring, DSO, DFC, the 28-year-old Lincolnshire farmer, had been my loyal companion since the blazing days of Normandy. I had never been to Woad Farm, but I knew every inch of it. His wife Sheila was expecting their first baby soon. He had been looking forward to that. I was devastated, and could no longer contain my grief.

The sky closed in and it began to snow again. The red berries that stood bright among the nearby hollies were the only colourful fragments in an otherwise melancholy scene. Even the tall black poplars seemed to be in mourning. It was so quiet I could hear the snow.

Two days later we were back at Gilze Rijen, where we buried Dring in the little graveyard near Breda. In my service career I had attended many funerals, some those of close friends, others of men who had passed through my life as strangers. All the funerals followed the same pattern: the slow march to the grave, the volley of shots from the firing party, the soul-searing notes from the bugle's Last Post. It was all so familiar.

The snow had followed us up from the Ardennes and it was a long, muffled, solemn procession. The padre's voice echoed back down the years, rising and falling with the whispered sighing of the nearby trees: 'Earth to earth, ashes to ashes, dust to dust ...' As I saluted Dring for the last time and the last bugle note faded in the distance, I could almost hear his laughter. See him smile. 'It's not the way I wanted it Scottie, but, as you know, in our game we seldom get a second chance.'

The war dragged on and we still suffered more than our share of losses, particularly supporting the Canadians in their drive through the Reichswald. 609 suffered the loss of yet another squadron commander when Eric Roberts was shot down and taken prisoner. His two flight commanders were not so lucky. Don Inches received severe burns while baling out and his fellow Australian, Flight Commander R. K. Gibson, was hit by flak and blew up with his rockets still aboard.

Wing Commander J. C. Button, DFC, was posted from 146 Wing to take the place of Dring. He had been a capable squadron commander, but the strain of the past months was beginning to take its toll on me and regrettably I ticked him off for appearing in my caravan in a dirty polo neck jersey. It was not the best of introductions, but John was one of those stout-hearted Englishmen who always bounced back, and when he did it was in more formal attire.

Some days later I was nearly shot down while attacking the telephone exchange in the centre of Wesel. My Typhoon was hit by flak and I had to make an emergency landing at Volkel, where my old 486 Squadron was now stationed in 122 Wing. They were flying Tempests with great success. Spike Umbers had returned to operations and was now its commanding officer. He drove me back to Gilze Rijen. I wanted him to stay the night but he preferred to return to his squadron for an early-morning show. The next day he was hit by flak while operating over the Meppen area. He crashed in flames and was killed.

On 24 March the operations order we had been waiting for arrived from 84 Group.

> Second British Army, with Second Canadian Corps under Command in conjunction with the IXth US Army and the First Allied Airborne Army will establish bridgeheads across the Rhine between Emmerich and Orsoy.

That morning I circled over Wesel in a Tempest and had a bird's-eye view of the whole show. The night before, at Montgomery's request, Wesel had been pulverized by Bomber Command and great clouds of smoke covered the remains of the town and large areas of the airborne dropping zone. Over 1,500 tugs and gliders blackened the skies over the flat country to the north of the Rhine and east of Emmerich. Parachutes began falling as thick as snowflakes and gliders dropped down through the haze and smoke like swarms of hungry locusts. It was an unforgettable sight—the might of the Allied air force. A number of aircraft crashed in flames. Others blew up in mid-air or fell slowly to the ground like flaming torches. Gliders losing a wing would spin down like sycamore seeds. Altogether 11,466 aircraft were engaged in the Rhine crossing, of which 108 were shot down. But the doorway to the Third Reich was thrust open and burning at its hinges.

With the last bastion now bridged and broken, and our feet on German soil, for me the war was virtually over. I received a notice posting me to the United Kingdom where I was later to join Transport Command. It had been a long and painful road from my early low-attack days at Tangmere to the waters of the Rhine. 'Jacko' Holmes had been killed soon after I had left for Hawkinge. Ian

Waddy and Alan Smith were still prisoners of war. 'Happy' Appleton and 'Woe' Wilson had both been shot down and badly injured. Spike Umbers, 'Bluey' Dall, Taylor-Cannon and Sergeant Powell were all killed within sight of the burning ruins of Hitler's Third Reich. Sheddan was brought down again, but escaped with a severe battering, and after a month in hospital courageously took to the skies again. 'Spud' Murphy and Jim McCaw had survived a number of hair-raising experiences, and were back production testing at Hawkers.

Some weeks later I lifted the wheels of my Typhoon from a liberated and now silent land and set course into the western sky towards England, the billowing cunims still reached up to the heavens like great white cathedrals. Ostend, Dunkirk and Calais slipped beneath. The English Channel, glistening like polished pewter, stretched out before me. Across its once-troubled waters the tall white ramparts of Beachy Head loomed into view. Brighton passed to starboard, and as I headed towards Tangmere I was seized by a deep yearning to stand again by the old dispersal hut, to listen back through the years for the sound of boyish laughter and the roar of our Typhoons.

Index

Bestselling War Fiction and Non-Fiction

☐ Passage to Mutiny	Alexander Kent	£2.50
☐ The Flag Captain	Alexander Kent	£2.50
☐ Badge of Glory	Douglas Reeman	£2.50
☐ Winged Escort	Douglas Reeman	£2.50
☐ Army of Shadows	John Harris	£2.50
☐ Up for Grabs	John Harris	£2.50
☐ Decoy	Dudley Pope	£1.95
☐ Curse of the Death's Head	Rupert Butler	£2.25
☐ Gestapo	Rupert Butler	£2.75
☐ Auschwitz and the Allies	Martin Gilbert	£4.95
☐ Tumult in the Clouds	James A. Goodson	£2.95
☐ Sigh for a Merlin	Alex Henshaw	£2.50
☐ Morning Glory	Stephen Howarth	£4.95
☐ The Doodlebugs	Norman Longmate	£4.95
☐ Colditz – The Full Story	Major P. Reid	£2.95

Bestselling Thriller/Suspense

☐ Voices on the Wind	Evelyn Anthony	£2.50
☐ See You Later, Alligator	William F. Buckley	£2.50
☐ Hell is Always Today	Jack Higgins	£1.75
☐ Brought in Dead	Harry Patterson	£1.95
☐ The Graveyard Shift	Harry Patterson	£1.95
☐ Maxwell's Train	Christopher Hyde	£2.50
☐ Russian Spring	Dennis Jones	£2.50
☐ Nightbloom	Herbert Lieberman	£2.50
☐ Basikasingo	John Matthews	£2.95
☐ The Secret Lovers	Charles McCarry	£2.50
☐ Fletch	Gregory Mcdonald	£1.95
☐ Green Monday	Michael M. Thomas	£2.95
☐ Someone Else's Money	Michael M. Thomas	£2.50
☐ Albatross	Evelyn Anthony	£2.50
☐ The Avenue of the Dead	Evelyn Anthony	£2.50

Bestselling Fiction

☐ Toll for the Brave	Jack Higgins	£1.75
☐ Basikasingo	John Matthews	£2.95
☐ Where No Man Cries	Emma Blair	£1.95
☐ Saudi	Laurie Devine	£2.95
☐ The Clogger's Child	Marie Joseph	£2.50
☐ The Gooding Girl	Pamela Oldfield	£2.75
☐ The Running Years	Claire Rayner	£2.75
☐ Duncton Wood	William Horwood	£3.50
☐ Aztec	Gary Jennings	£3.95
☐ Enemy in Sight	Alexander Kent	£2.50
☐ Strumpet City	James Plunkett	£3.50
☐ The Volunteers	Douglas Reeman	£2.50
☐ The Second Lady	Irving Wallace	£2.50
☐ The Assassin	Evelyn Anthony	£2.50
☐ The Pride	Judith Saxton	£2.50

ARROW BOOKS, BOOKSERVICE BY POST, PO BOX 29, DOUGLAS, ISLE OF MAN, BRITISH ISLES

NAME ....

ADDRESS ....

....

....

Please enclose a cheque or postal order made out to Arrow Books Ltd. for the amount due and allow the following for postage and packing.

U.K. CUSTOMERS: Please allow 22p per book to a maximum of £3.00.

B.F.P.O. & EIRE: Please allow 22p per book to a maximum of £3.00.

OVERSEAS CUSTOMERS: Please allow 22p per book.

Whilst every effort is made to keep prices low it is sometimes necessary to increase cover prices at short notice. Arrow Books reserve the right to show new retail prices on covers which may differ from those previously advertised in the text or elsewhere.

Bestselling Fiction

☐ Toll for the Brave	Jack Higgins	£1.75
☐ Basikasingo	John Matthews	£2.95
☐ Where No Man Cries	Emma Blair	£1.95
☐ Saudi	Laurie Devine	£2.95
☐ The Clogger's Child	Marie Joseph	£2.50
☐ The Gooding Girl	Pamela Oldfield	£2.75
☐ The Running Years	Claire Rayner	£2.75
☐ Duncton Wood	William Horwood	£3.50
☐ Aztec	Gary Jennings	£3.95
☐ Enemy in Sight	Alexander Kent	£2.50
☐ Strumpet City	James Plunkett	£3.50
☐ The Volunteers	Douglas Reeman	£2.50
☐ The Second Lady	Irving Wallace	£2.50
☐ The Assassin	Evelyn Anthony	£2.50
☐ The Pride	Judith Saxton	£2.50

ARROW BOOKS, BOOKSERVICE BY POST, PO BOX 29, DOUGLAS, ISLE OF MAN, BRITISH ISLES

NAME ....

ADDRESS ....

....

....

Please enclose a cheque or postal order made out to Arrow Books Ltd. for the amount due and allow the following for postage and packing.

U.K. CUSTOMERS: Please allow 22p per book to a maximum of £3.00.

B.F.P.O. & EIRE: Please allow 22p per book to a maximum of £3.00.

OVERSEAS CUSTOMERS: Please allow 22p per book.

Whilst every effort is made to keep prices low it is sometimes necessary to increase cover prices at short notice. Arrow Books reserve the right to show new retail prices on covers which may differ from those previously advertised in the text or elsewhere.

Bestselling Non-Fiction

☐ The Alexander Principle	Wilfred Barlow	£2.95
☐ The Complete Book of Exercises	Diagram Group	£4.95
☐ Everything is Negotiable	Gavin Kennedy	£2.95
☐ Health on Your Plate	Janet Pleshette	£2.50
☐ The Cheiro Book of Fate and Fortune	Cheiro	£2.95
☐ The Handbook of Chinese Horoscopes	Theodora Lau	£2.50
☐ Hollywood Babylon	Kenneth Anger	£7.95
☐ Hollywood Babylon II	Kenneth Anger	£7.95
☐ The Domesday Heritage	Ed. Elizabeth Hallam	£3.95
☐ Historic Railway Disasters	O. S. Nock	£2.50
☐ Wildlife of the Domestic Cat	Roger Tabor	£4.50
☐ Elvis and Me	Priscilla Presley	£2.95
☐ Maria Callas	Arianna Stassinopoulos	£2.50
☐ The Brendan Voyage	Tim Severin	£3.50

ARROW BOOKS, BOOKSERVICE BY POST, PO BOX 29, DOUGLAS, ISLE OF MAN, BRITISH ISLES

NAME ....

ADDRESS ....

....

....

Please enclose a cheque or postal order made out to Arrow Books Ltd. for the amount due and allow the following for postage and packing.

U.K. CUSTOMERS: Please allow 22p per book to a maximum of £3.00.

B.F.P.O. & EIRE: Please allow 22p per book to a maximum of £3.00.

OVERSEAS CUSTOMERS: Please allow 22p per book.

Whilst every effort is made to keep prices low it is sometimes necessary to increase cover prices at short notice. Arrow Books reserve the right to show new retail prices on covers which may differ from those previously advertised in the text or elsewhere.

Bestselling Non-Fiction

☐ The Gradual Vegetarian	Lisa Tracy	£2.95
☐ The Food Scandal	Caroline Walker & Geoffrey Cannon	£3.95
☐ Harmony Rules	Gary Butt & Frena Bloomfield	£2.25
☐ Everything is Negotiable	Gavin Kennedy	£2.95
☐ Hollywood Babylon	Kevin Anger	£7.95
☐ Red Watch	Gordon Honeycombe	£2.75
☐ Wildlife of the Domestic Cat	Roger Tabor	£4.50
☐ The World of Placido Domingo	Daniel Snowman	£4.95
☐ The Sinbad Voyage	Tim Severin	£2.75
☐ The Hills is Lonely	Lillian Beckwith	£1.95
☐ English Country Cottage	R. J. Brown	£3.50
☐ Raw Energy	Leslie & Susannah Kenton	£2.95

A Selection of Arrow Bestsellers

☐ Voices on the Wind	Evelyn Anthony	£2.50
☐ Someone Else's Money	Michael M. Thomas	£2.50
☐ The Executioner's Song	Norman Mailer	£3.50
☐ The Alexander Principle	Wilfred Barlow	£2.95
☐ Everything is Negotiable	Gavin Kennedy	£2.95
☐ The New Girlfriend & other stories	Ruth Rendell	£1.95
☐ An Unkindness of Ravens	Ruth Rendell	£1.95
☐ Dead in the Morning	Margaret Yorke	£1.75
☐ The Domesday Heritage	Ed. Elizabeth Hallam	£3.95
☐ Elvis and Me	Priscilla Presley	£2.95
☐ The World of Placido Domingo	Daniel Snowman	£4.95
☐ Maria Callas	Arianna Stassinopoulos	£2.50
☐ The Brendan Voyage	Tim Severin	£3.50
☐ A Shine of Rainbows	Lillian Beckwith	£1.95
☐ Rates of Exchange	Malcolm Bradbury	£2.95
☐ Thy Tears Might Cease	Michael Farrell	£2.95
☐ Pudding and Pie (Nancy Mitford Omnibus)	Nancy Mitford	£3.95

ARROW BOOKS, BOOKSERVICE BY POST, PO BOX 29, DOUGLAS, ISLE OF MAN, BRITISH ISLES

NAME ....

ADDRESS ....

....

....

Please enclose a cheque or postal order made out to Arrow Books Ltd. for the amount due and allow the following for postage and packing.

U.K. CUSTOMERS: Please allow 22p per book to a maximum of £3.00.

B.F.P.O. & EIRE: Please allow 22p per book to a maximum of £3.00.

OVERSEAS CUSTOMERS: Please allow 22p per book.

Whilst every effort is made to keep prices low it is sometimes necessary to increase cover prices at short notice. Arrow Books reserve the right to show new retail prices on covers which may differ from those previously advertised in the text or elsewhere.